PENGUIN BOOKS

natural
nourishing
recipes

PENELOPE SACH is Australia's leading practitioner of naturopathic, homeopathic and herbal medicine. She runs a highly successful clinic in Sydney and produces her own range of organically grown herbal teas. Her most recent books include *Detox*, *Natural Woman*, *Natural Men's Health* and *Natural Children's Health*.

For more about Penelope Sach,
visit www.penelopesach.com.au

Other titles by Penelope Sach

Healing and Cleansing with Herbal Tea
Natural Woman
Detox
The Little Book of Wellbeing
Take Care of Yourself
Natural Men's Health
Natural Children's Health

natural
nourishing
recipes

PENELOPE SACH

PENGUIN BOOKS

PENGUIN BOOKS

Published by the Penguin Group
Penguin Group (Australia)
250 Camberwell Road, Camberwell, Victoria 3124, Australia
(a division of Pearson Australia Group Pty Ltd)
Penguin Group (USA) Inc.
375 Hudson Street, New York, New York 10014, USA
Penguin Group (Canada)
90 Eglinton Avenue East, Suite 700, Toronto, ON M4P 2Y3, Canada
(a division of Pearson Penguin Canada Inc.)
Penguin Books Ltd
80 Strand, London WC2R 0RL, England
Penguin Ireland
25 St Stephen's Green, Dublin 2, Ireland
(a division of Penguin Books Ltd)
Penguin Books India Pvt Ltd
11 Community Centre, Panchsheel Park, New Delhi – 110 017, India
Penguin Group (NZ)
Cnr Airborne and Rosedale Roads, Albany, Auckland, New Zealand
(a division of Pearson New Zealand Ltd)
Penguin Books (South Africa) (Pty) Ltd
24 Sturdee Avenue, Rosebank, Johannesburg 2196, South Africa

Penguin Books Ltd, Registered Offices: 80 Strand, London, WC2R 0RL, England

First published by Penguin Group (Australia), a division of Pearson Australia Group Pty Ltd, 2006

1 3 5 7 9 10 8 6 4 2

Copyright © Penelope Sach 2006

Design by Elizabeth Dias © Penguin Group (Australia)
Cover photograph by Julie Anne Renouf
Author photograph © Louise Lister
Typeset in ITC Legacy Serif by Post Pre-press Group, Brisbane, Queensland
Printed and bound in Australia by McPherson's Printing Group, Maryborough, Victoria

National Library of Australia
Cataloguing-in-Publication data:

Sach, Penelope.
Natural nourishing recipes.

Includes index.
ISBN-13: 978 0 143 00467 7.
ISBN-10: 0 143 00467 0.

1. Cookery (Natural foods). I. Title.

641.5637

www.penguin.com.au

Contents

Natural recipes for healing

This is not a fancy recipe book. It is a reminder of healthy, simple eating, with dishes you can prepare with little time and no fuss, according to your individual health needs. I have focused on foods that are nourishing in every way – foods that make you feel good and give you energy to get you through each day. When we eat quality protein, fruit, vegetables, grains, salads, nuts, seeds, water, herbal teas and raw juices, and combine them with small amounts of fats, and throw herbs and spices in to enhance the flavours, we are feeding and nourishing every cell of our body.

The simple ideas and meals I discuss in this book have been with me for a long time. Some I have been using since I was a student; it was always my house that all my student friends, and later my professional and family friends, enjoyed coming to for a meal. Many of my girlfriends used to say that I had a way of throwing vegetables together that they had never tasted before – all I did was steam a variety of colours, melt a dob of butter through them and add a sprinkle of sea salt or vegetable salt. It became known as 'Penelope's vegetables', and often we would eat big plates of these vegetables or munch on a fresh garden salad with nuts or eggs tossed through while we watched a video.

When I became a consulting naturopath many of my clients asked me how they could best prepare vegetables or a salad. I am always willing to share what I do, and my clients and friends love the simplicity of the ideas. All too often I see diligent mothers trying to cope with gourmet cookbook recipes and becoming disillusioned by the preparation and time required. They often end up abandoning their simple healthy ways of preparing vegetables, salads, protein and grains.

I am continually concerned by how many people – single, married, old, young – still do not know how to throw together a healthy salad, pasta or roast dinner, or even know how to cook basic grains. It really is easy to learn these basics and create a range of interesting, nourishing and delicious food for yourself and your family. That's why I have written this book: to share with you the recipes I have been cooking for years. With these recipes you can prepare a home-cooked meal in the shortest time possible and feel the benefits of natural flavours, have more time with your family and save money on takeaway and restaurant food.

Fad diets have made everything so complicated these days, whereas the rules for staying healthy and nourished are actually simple. And they are worthwhile. Healing the body and mind through pure, delicious foods will prevent long-term illness as well as aches, pains, mood swings, fatigue, irritability, depression and all manner of other modern-day health problems. We need to go back to basics in cooking at home, eating regularly and gathering the family for balanced meals; and we must try to balance our temptation to eat rich, processed foods and quick takeaways. Naturally, you will occasionally be tempted to eat a rich dessert or have a chocolate treat. I always say that life is about balance: 90 per cent good and 10 per cent naughty. Enjoy the 'naughty', but use it as a treat once or twice a week, and the next day try to get back on track by eating cleansing foods such as soup, fruit, juice and vegetables.

In my work many people ask me about the effectiveness of the high-protein, low-carbohydrate diets that seem to be everywhere these days. These eating plans will help you lose weight and cut down your intake of refined carbohydrates such as fizzy drinks, bread, pasta, desserts, alcohol, cakes, biscuits and pastries. Unfortunately, however, on these diets many people cut out carbohydrates and vegetables altogether. My advice is to focus your carbohydrate intake on the unrefined 'good' carbohydrates such as multigrain breads, brown rice, buckwheat, oats and legumes. If you vary these daily, your health and energy levels will be sustained.

It is important to be creative and flexible in your cooking. If, for example, I have suggested vegetables you don't like, simply exchange them for others of the same colour. I have included recipes for red and white meat, but many of the other dishes are suitable for vegetarians. You don't have to go out and buy exotic ingredients, because taking care of yourself and eating well should be inexpensive and easy. It's about lifestyle and balance.

See the Quick reference guide to healthy cooking (pp 17–28) to find the recipes suitable to your health needs.

❧ Breakfast, lunch and dinner

Our busy lives mean that we are working long hours, with no proper break during the day, and we need all the energy and alertness we can muster. Food gives us fuel, just like petrol to a car; unless we 'pump' energy into our body during each busy day, we cannot expect our engine to perform efficiently.

Breakfast and lunch should be our main meals of the day, with dinner still nourishing but lighter, with less carbohydrate. Or, if you simply cannot find time for a full breakfast – or if you feel heavy or acidic on a large breakfast – a lighter breakfast with a mid-morning snack might suit the rhythm of your digestion more.

A nourishing lunch, whether eaten at home, brought to work or purchased during the work day is also a vital step to continued good health. I have seen many people, particularly men, transformed in their energy levels and mental power by this one simple change in their lifestyle. I hope you glance at the ideas in this book and feel inspired to start taking a delicious lunch to work with you. For a start, you can easily enjoy some wholemeal grains (soaked in boiling water in a thermos the night before; see pages 50–51), with tuna, chicken or egg and a salad, a piece of fruit and a small bag of nuts; or a nutritious sandwich on Lavash bread (see page 84) and a fresh juice; or a simple noodle soup (see Cleansing Noodle Soup on page 73) with a salad on the side – these options are all far superior to a fatty takeaway hamburger and French fries. And in winter, when we need hot food and more carbohydrate to get us through the day, why not enjoy soup (again, prepared the night before and stored in a thermos, or heated in the microwave at work; see any of the recipes in the soup section, pp 71–74) with crusty grainy bread on the side? Or if you are eating out in winter you can easily enjoy a hot casserole, or a big bowl of thick, nourishing soup with legumes or chicken, or a curry with rice.

Our evening meals can be very heavy. When you sleep, all of your body needs to sleep, including your digestive system. It can't do this if you go to bed on a full, heavy stomach; you can have a disturbed, restless night and your vital force or energy levels will be low the next morning. I believe this is also a recipe for disaster if you are trying to lose weight. Food 'sitting' in your digestive system and bowel all night has to find areas to 'rest' too and will turn into fat, so if you are trying to shed a few excess kilos, try the lighter dinners in this book. Do not eat pasta, bread or rice in the evening; stick to a light protein such as fish, eggs, tofu or chicken with lots of vegetables (just a little potato – a carbohydrate – if you love them). Try to eat dinner at least three to four hours before you go to bed.

We all fight the clock for time in our vastly different lifestyles and busy schedules, but by organising your pantry with the essentials (see page 11), buying fresh vegetables on a regular basis and using your creativity, cooking can become not only a delight, but relaxing and rewarding. It will allow you more time with your partner and children, you will feel better in all parts of your health and most of all you will feel nourished in every way.

Foods for the sexes

When it comes to food tastes and cravings, men and women are quite different. I recommend you use this book in conjunction with my previous books, *Natural Woman* and *Natural Men's Health*, to really give your body the best possible treatment.

Women's cycles strongly affect their food choices, and for families in which the woman is responsible for shopping and preparing meals, this can affect the entire family's food intake.

Before and during a period, women often crave iron-rich foods (as part of the natural cycle of the womb requiring more blood in preparation for a fertilised egg) and may prepare meat dishes and green vegetables such as spinach, broccoli and bok choy. From ovulation (approximately 10–14 days after the period) onwards, women's cravings for carbohydrates and sugars increase, and these are the times you may see more potatoes, pasta, bread and chocolate desserts as part of family meals. During this ovulation-to-period time, particularly 3–4 days before the period, women may drink more alcohol to satisfy their sugar cravings, and the alcohol may affect them quickly. With these cravings and hormonal swings the stomach and abdomen can become bloated, and fluid retention and irritability are exacerbated by even more sugar cravings.

If any of the above is familiar to you, I recommend that you accept the cravings as part of your cycle, but try to choose the better-quality carbohydrates such as grainy bread and brown rice, and unrefined sugars such as fresh fruits rather than the refined sugars found in junk food that will leave you feeling even more bloated. A good option for sugar cravings is stewed or cooked fruits, because the acid is removed and they are very sweet; this way you will satisfy your cravings but the bloating in your stomach will be minimal.

Men, on the other hand, are influenced by their testosterone. They generally weigh more and have a heavier muscle build than women, which affects what – and how much – they like to eat.

Men tend to enjoy protein (particularly red meat) and carbohydrate, but vegetables and salads are often at the bottom of the list. In recent studies it has been found how important folic acid is not only for pre-pregnancy and early pregnancy in women to prevent spina bifida in their baby, but also for men to regulate homocysteine (a toxic amino acid by-product) levels, and in preventing Alzheimer's and heart disease. In order to get more of this vital folic acid men can choose from a wide variety of healthy foods, including broccoli, brussels sprouts, wholegrains, root vegetables, asparagus, sunflower seeds, oysters, liver, meats and citrus fruits.

Men often eat a light breakfast and lunch and then overeat meat and carbohydrates at dinner, causing fermentation in the bowel, a sluggish liver and leaving them tired the next morning. By focusing on breakfast and lunch and a lighter evening meal, you will feel more satisfied and have maximum energy. Men often need a protein milkshake once or twice through the day if they are exercising. I also recommend a rehydration – electrolyte – drink during or before exercise to keep muscles from cramping.

Be careful not to binge on wine with your evening meal as a way to relax and unwind. Each glass is loaded with sugar and can be a weight enhancer and can cause disturbed sleep and apnoea. To get out of this bad habit, try to have two or three alcohol-free nights each week, and try alternating wine evenings with a vodka and tonic or Campari and soda, neither of which is overloaded with sugar.

Foods to lift the spirits

The food we eat can have a powerful impact on the way we feel. Sometimes it is difficult to discern exactly which foods we are allergic to or feel 'down' on, and which foods can help lift our spirits.

Unfortunately some people do suffer from biochemical depression, which is constant and severe, and needs to be diagnosed by a qualified physician. Situational depression is different. It affects most people at some time or another, during which normal reactions to external events can be affected by PMS (premenstrual syndrome), hypoglycaemia, stress, trauma, pesticides, allergies and certain pharmaceutical drugs. Our moods are also affected by feel-good hormones such as serotonin, melatonin, dopamine, epinephrine (adrenaline) and norepinephrine (noradrenaline) – referred to as neurotransmitters. These are enhanced by doing exercise, feeling good about ourselves, falling in love and eating healthy foods.

In some people, particularly those with allergies, poor digestion, high stress and PMS, these chemicals are depleted and need to be replenished through added herbs and vitamins, including St John's wort (for mild depression), liquorice (for sugar levels), Siberian ginseng (tonic for energy), ginkgo biloba (for short-term memory), damiana (to boost men's libido), ginger (for circulation), cayenne (for energy), kava kava (for anxiety), valerian (for insomnia), oats (tonic) and bacopa (for long-term memory). (You will see a more detailed discussion of these in my books *Natural Woman* and *Natural Men's Health*.) As a herbalist I often prescribe these herbs for patients who may need an extra boost during long working hours, or who are fatigued, or who generally eat well but still suffer some effects of stress, anxiety or lowered libido.

We all need vitamin B and minerals such as magnesium, calcium and phosphorus, so I have included many recipes that include these essentials, especially fresh foods such as vegetables, fruit, wholegrains, fish and meat. I have also included an introduction to each recipe to let you know the benefits of the foods included, and to help you tailor your eating to obtain optimum goodness for your body and mind.

What to have in your cupboard and/or refrigerator

Cupboard
sea salt, black peppercorns, white pepper, honey, free-range eggs, peanut butter, almond paste, organic jam

Dried herbs and spices
cinnamon, nutmeg, sage, rosemary, mint, basil, oregano, parsley, mixed herbs, chilli powder, curry powder

Grains
brown rice (organic is best), Arborio (risotto) rice, roasted buckwheat, rolled oats or rice oats

Bulbs and vegetables
garlic, ginger, onions, potatoes, pumpkin, sweet potato, carrots

Fresh fruit
apples, oranges, grapes, watermelon, peaches, apricots

Legumes
azuki beans, lima beans, borlotti beans, red and brown lentils

Oils
olive oil, vegetable oil, sesame oil

Canned foods
tomatoes (whole and diced), tuna, salmon, sardines, baked beans

Pasta
spaghetti, farfalle, fettuccini

Noodles
buckwheat, egg, wholemeal

Refrigerator

wholegrain, Dijon and English mustard
organic tea – black, green or herbal (see my list of herbal teas on
pages 43–44)
good-quality ground coffee

Sauces
tamari sauce, soy sauce

Vegetables
broccoli, beans, peas, bok choy, spinach

Freezer
free-range chicken
your favourite cuts of lamb and beef
home-cooked minestrone soup (see page 72)
frozen peas
soy ice-cream
stock – vegetable, chicken and fish (see pages 75–76)
herbal tea ice blocks (see page 42)

Fruits, vegetables and soy beans contain active plant
chemicals called polyphenols. The red pigment in
grapes, cherries, berries, plums and red cabbage
helps fight heart disease and keep the lungs and
blood vessels healthy. Studies have found strong
links between the carotenoids in yellow and orange
vegetables and cancer prevention. Other active
substances in mushrooms and oysters have been
found to enhance the immune system.

12 simple steps to good nutrition

1   Wherever possible use fresh herbs, spices and natural minerals such as parsley, basil and thyme, garlic, ginger, seaweed, sea salt, lemongrass and turmeric.

2   Steam, bake, casserole or sauté foods to retain their living enzymes and nutritional values, and also eat raw vegetables and salads daily.

3   Use varieties of proteins such as legumes, fish, eggs, nuts and seeds, and moderate amounts of red and white meat.

4   Consume raw, cooked or juiced fresh fruit and vegetables daily.

5   Incorporate complex carbohydrates 2–3 times a day, such as brown rice, buckwheat, grainy wholemeal breads, whole wheat and oat porridge. For a balanced meal, combine wholegrains with beans or legumes for a full protein.

6   Experiment with sprouts from grains and vegetables (you can buy these at your local grocer), because they are high in enzymes, minerals and amino acids.

7   Include naturally fermented products such as yoghurt, miso and soy sauce in your diet.

8   Try tasting and using different sources of calcium, such as whole milk, rice milk, soy milk, goat's milk and cheese.

9   Always include green vegetables or greens from barley, wheat grass or spirulina for their high content of chlorophyll, the 'magic' substance formed by the sun on plants and an invaluable source of vitamin A and C, and to regulate calcium metabolism.

10   Include orange vegetables and fruit daily for their high active anti-oxidant content, which reduces and prevents free radical (toxin) damage.

11   Drink fresh, filtered water daily; at least 2 litres (8 glasses). You can add organic herbal tea to the water for a dual healing effect.

12   Eat slowly and happily, and embrace the fullness of life.

As Hippocrates said, 'Let food be your medicine and medicine your food.' Our body is a wonderful machine. It needs water, oil, cleanliness and respect. It will then perform at its best. Try one step at a time, and feel the life force of your body drinking from the life forces of nature.

※ *Milk: good or bad?*

Dairy products (milk, cheese, yoghurt) are a truly wonderful natural source of calcium, but many people are sensitive to the protein lactose and so have stopped eating dairy altogether.

If you do not get bloating or mucus after eating dairy, you may be perfectly all right on dairy. Yoghurt and buttermilk are very easily digested by most people because the lactose has been broken down in the fermentation process. Yoghurt is especially good because it contains natural bacteria that promote healthy intestinal bacteria in the bowel, which is vital for keeping free-radical damage at bay.

If you are allergic to cow's milk, goat's milk is easier to digest and is a complete protein. Soy milk is made from soy beans and can be quite heavy on the digestion. It is not high in calcium, but some manufacturers add small amounts of calcium. Rice milk, made from white rice, is also an option if you like a milky taste on your cereal, and again calcium is generally added.

Quick reference guide to healthy cooking

Use this guide to find the recipes suitable to your health needs.

Anaemia (low iron)

Angela's spinach and cheese bake *p 96*

Beetroot and asparagus salad *p 68*

Butter bean, potato and spinach salad *p 60*

Carrot and beetroot juice *p 32*

Carrot, spinach and beet greens juice *p 34*

Cherry juice *p 39*

Jamie's osso bucco with parsnip mash *p 102*

Jamie's Thai beef salad *p 106*

Lamb and lentils on a bed of mashed potato *p 121*

Lamb casserole *p 129*

Mixed salad with nuts *p 58*

Muscat grape juice *p 38*

Spinach and rice *p 100*

Arthritis

Avocado, mint and pea salad *p 57*

Baked apples and pears *p 135*

Barramundi, lemon and potato *p 104*

Butter bean rissoles *p 120*

Carrot and celery juice *p 32*

Carrot and ginger juice *p 33*

Carrot, beetroot and ginger juice *p 33*

Cherry juice *p 39*

Couscous salad *p 64*

Fish with soy sauce and ginger *p 113*

Jamie's whole sardines with roasted garlic, olive and fennel salad *p 62*

Arthritis *(cont...)*

Kingfish with fresh mint sauce
 p 130

Maria's peasant-style chicken with
  rosemary *p 98*

Minestrone soup *p 72*

Pan-fried salmon   *p 95*

Poached Pears   *p 133*

Rice salad   *p 54*

Stone fruit salad   *p 45*

Whole baked snapper   *p 109*

Asthma

Beetroot and asparagus salad   *p 68*

Buckwheat pancakes   *p 46*

Butter bean rissoles   *p 120*

Carrot and ginger juice   *p 33*

Chicken and vegetable casserole   *p 101*

Citrus fruit salad   *p 45*

Jamie's whole sardines with roasted
  garlic, olive and fennel salad   *p 62*

Kingfish with fresh mint sauce   *p 130*

Lamb and lentils on a bed of mashed
  potato   *p 121*

Lamb casserole   *p 129*

Peach, apricot and mango juice
 p 38

Poached pears   *p 133*

Rice salad   *p 54*

Salmon rice rissoles   *p 123*

Stone fruit salad   *p 45*

Summer Delight tea   *p 44*

Tofu and shiitake mushroom stir-fry
 p 110

Whole baked snapper   *p 109*

Cholesterol

Apple juice   *p 40*

Avocado, mint and pea salad   *p 57*

Barramundi, lemon and potato   *p 104*

Butter bean, potato and spinach salad
 p 60

Carrot and celery juice   *p 32*

Cauliflower and broccoli soup   *p 74*

Chickpea and avocado salad   *p 61*

Citrus fruit salad   *p 45*

Energy porridge   *p 50*

Fish with soy sauce and ginger   *p 113*

Homemade muesli   *p 50*

Jamie's whole sardines with roasted
  garlic, olive and fennel salad   *p 62*

Kingfish with fresh mint sauce   *p 130*

Oatmeal porridge   *p 49*

Pan-fried salmon   *p 95*

Pearl perch with Corn Flakes crusty
  coating   *p 128*

Rice salad   *p 54*

Salmon rice rissoles   *p 123*

Whole baked snapper   *p 109*

Circulation

Beetroot and asparagus salad   *p 68*

Carrot, beetroot and ginger juice   *p 33*

Citrus fruit salad   *p 45*

Fish with soy sauce and ginger   *p 113*

Kingfish with fresh mint sauce   *p 130*

Lamb and lentils on a bed of mashed potato   *p 121*

Maria's peasant-style chicken with rosemary   *p 98*

Prawns with Asian herbs   *p 122*

Scrambled curried eggs   *p 51*

Spaghetti with garlic, oil and chilli   *p 108*

Concentration

Buckwheat pancakes   *p 46*

Butter bean, potato and spinach salad   *p 60*

Carrot, beetroot and ginger juice   *p 33*

Chickpea and avocado salad   *p 61*

Egg and asparagus salad   *p 59*

Energy porridge   *p 50*

Fish with soy sauce and ginger   *p 113*

Jamie's lentil and bacon salad   *p 56*

Jamie's osso bucco with parsnip mash   *p 102*

Kingfish with fresh mint sauce   *p 130*

Maria's peasant-style chicken with rosemary   *p 98*

Muscat grape juice   *p 38*

Oatmeal porridge   *p 49*

Pan-fried salmon   *p 95*

Peach, apricot and mango juice   *p 38*

Rice salad   *p 54*

Salmon rice rissoles   *p 123*

Spinach and rice   *p 100*

Stone fruit salad   *p 45*

The healthy omelette   *p 52*

Tuna macaroni   *p 99*

Whole baked snapper   *p 109*

Depression and irritability

Anzac biscuits   *p 134*

Apres tea   *p 43*

Baked sweet bananas with cinnamon   *p 132*

Barramundi, lemon and potato   *p 104*

Couscous salad   *p 64*

Energy porridge   *p 50*

Fish with soy sauce and ginger   *p 113*

Homemade muesli   *p 50*

Jamie's osso bucco with parsnip mash   *p 102*

Jamie's Thai beef salad   *p 106*

Depression and irritability *(cont...)*

Detox/liver

Digestive problems/ulcers/heartburn

Fluid retention/sluggish kidneys/kidney stones

Gluten-free

Hyperactivity

Hypoglycaemia (low blood sugar)

Hypoglycaemia (low blood sugar) *(cont...)*

Butter bean, potato and spinach salad
p 60

Cheese, tomato and basil pizza   *p 86*

Cherry juice   *p 39*

Chicken and vegetable casserole   *p 101*

Chicken drumsticks   *p 118*

Chickpea and avocado salad   *p 61*

Chickpea spread   *p 79*

Couscous salad   *p 64*

Energy porridge   *p 50*

Homemade muesli   *p 50*

Jamie's lentil and bacon salad   *p 56*

Jamie's osso bucco with parsnip mash
p 102

Jamie's Thai beef salad   *p 106*

Jamie's whole sardines with roasted
garlic, olive and fennel salad   *p 62*

Kebabs   *p 112*

Lamb and lentils on a bed of mashed
potato   *p 121*

Lamb casserole   *p 129*

Maria's peasant-style chicken with
rosemary   *p 98*

Mixed salad with nuts   *p 58*

Mulberry, blackberry, raspberry and
cranberry juice   *p 40*

My favourite antipasto platter   *p 87*

My favourite Caesar salad   *p 66*

Oatmeal porridge   *p 49*

Orange, pineapple, lemon and
grapefruit juice   *p 37*

Potato, onion and cheese bake   *p 88*

Prawns with Asian herbs   *p 122*

Rice salad   *p 54*

Roast spatchcock   *p 114*

Salmon rice rissoles   *p 123*

Soy chicken and potatoes   *p 125*

Spaghetti vongole   *p 124*

Spinach and rice   *p 100*

Tahini   *p 80*

Tasty grated onion and potato cakes *p 90*

Tasty sandwiches   *p 84*

The healthy omelette   *p 52*

Tofu and shiitake mushroom stir-fry *p 110*

Triple E tea   *p 44*

Tuna macaroni   *p 99*

Vegetable rissoles   *p 116*

Wholemeal pancakes   *p 48*

Immune system (coughs, colds, flus)

Baked apples and pears   *p 135*

Baked sweet bananas with cinnamon
p 132

Barramundi, lemon and potato   *p 104*

Carrot and ginger juice   *p 33*

Citrus fruit salad   *p 45*

Immune system (coughs, colds, flus) (cont...)

Jamie's whole sardines with toasted
   garlic, olive and fennel salad *p 62*
Kingfish with fresh mint sauce *p 130*
Lamb casserole *p 129*
Orange and lemon juice *p 36*
Orange, pineapple, lemon and
   grapefruit juice *p 37*

Stone fruit salad *p 45*
Strawberry, kiwifruit and white grape
   juice *p 39*
Tofu and shiitake mushroom stir-fry
   p 110
Whole baked snapper *p 109*

Insomnia

Apres tea *p 43*
Energy porridge *p 50*

Oatmeal porridge *p 49*
Petal tea *p 43*

Irritable bowel

Anzac biscuits *p 134*
Apricot coconut balls *p 131*
Bakes apples and pears *p 135*
Butter bean rissoles *p 120*
Carrot and ginger juice *p 33*
Homemade muesli *p 50*
Jamie's lentil and bacon salad *p 56*
Minestrone soup *p 72*
Pan-fried salmon *p 95*
Peach, apricot and mango juice *p 38*

Pear juice *p 41*
Poached pears *p 133*
Potato and sweet potato wedges *p 85*
Prawns with Asian herbs *p 122*
Pumpkin and sage pasta *p 126*
Spaghetti vongole *p 124*
Spinach and rice *p 100*
Stone fruit salad *p 45*
Vegetable rissoles *p 116*
Whole baked snapper *p 109*

Libido

Cheese, tomato and basil pizza *p 86*
Chicken and vegetable casserole *p 101*
Energy porridge *p 50*
Jamie's osso bucco with parsnip mash
   p 102

Lamb and lentils on a bed of mashed
   potato *p 121*
Lamb casserole *p 129*
Muscat grape juice *p 38*
Oatmeal porridge *p 49*

Libido *(cont . . .)*

Pan-fried salmon   *p 95*

Peach, apricot and mango juice   *p 38*

Stone fruit salad   *p 45*

The healthy omelette   *p 52*

PMT

Angela's spinach and cheese bake   *p 96*

Anzac biscuits   *p 134*

Apricot coconut balls   *p 131*

Baked apples and pears   *p 135*

Baked sweet bananas with cinnamon
   p 132

Butter bean, potato and spinach salad
   p 60

Carrot, celery and parsley juice   *p 34*

Chicken and vegetable casserole   *p 101*

Couscous salad   *p 64*

Egg and asparagus salad   *p 59*

Lamb and lentils on a bed of mashed
   potato   *p 121*

Maria's peasant-style chicken with
   rosemary   *p 98*

Minestrone soup   *p 72*

My favourite antipasto platter   *p 87*

My favourite Caesar salad   *p 66*

Pan-fried salmon   *p 95*

Poached pears   *p 133*

Pumpkin and sage pasta   *p 126*

Rice salad   *p 54*

Roast spatchcock   *p 114*

The healthy omelette   *p 52*

Tofu and shiitake mushroom stir-fry *p 110*

Tuna macaroni   *p 99*

Watermelon juice   *p 41*

Prostate

Apricot coconut balls   *p 131*

Barley soup   *p 71*

Cheese, tomato and basil pizza   *p 86*

Chicken and vegetable casserole
   p 101

Lamb casserole   *p 129*

Minestrone soup   *p 72*

Mulberry, blackberry, raspberry and
   cranberry juice   *p 40*

Pan-fried salmon   *p 95*

Stone fruit salad   *p 45*

Tuna macaroni   *p 99*

Rheumatism (muscle pain)

Baked apples and pears   *p 135*

Barramundi, lemon and potato   *p 104*

Butter bean rissoles   *p 120*

Butterfly zucchini pasta   *p 105*

Rheumatism (muscle pain) (cont...)

Carrot and celery juice *p 32*
Cherry juice *p 39*
Chicken and vegetable casserole *p 101*
Couscous salad *p 64*
Fish with soy sauce and ginger *p 113*
Jamie's whole sardines with roasted
    garlic, olive and fennel salad *p 62*
Kingfish with fresh mint sauce *p 130*

Maria's peasant-style chicken with
    rosemary *p 98*
Minestrone soup *p 72*
Pearl perch with Corn Flakes crusty
    coating *p 128*
Poached pears *p 133*
Rice salad *p 54*
Stone fruit salad *p 45*

Skin – acne

Barramundi, lemon and potato *p 104*
Carrot and beetroot juice *p 32*
Carrot, spinach and beet greens juice
    p 34
Chickpea and avocado salad *p 61*
Couscous salad *p 64*

Kingfish with fresh mint sauce
    p 130
Minestrone soup *p 72*
Peach, apricot and mango juice *p 38*
Vegetable rissoles *p 116*
Whole baked snapper *p 109*

Skin – dry

Avocado, mint and pea salad *p 57*
Baked apples and pears *p 135*
Barramundi, lemon and potato *p 104*
Carrot, spinach and beet greens juice
    p 34
Minestrone soup *p 72*
Mixed salad with nuts *p 58*

Pan-fried salmon *p 95*
Peach, apricot and mango juice *p 38*
Pearl perch with Corn Flakes crusty
    coating *p 128*
Poached pears *p 133*
Spinach and rice *p 100*
Whole baked snapper *p 109*

Sports energy

Angela's spinach and cheese bake *p 96*
Anzac biscuits *p 134*
Apricot coconut balls *p 131*

Baked sweet bananas with cinnamon
    p 132
Barley soup *p 71*

Wheat- and yeast-free recipes

Juices

Raw vegetable juices

Raw juice is one of the finest ways to cleanse your body quickly, give back living enzymes essential to healthy cell growth, and dilute free radical (toxin) damage. It is also a delicious snack.

I recommend 1 large glass (approximately 250 ml) of raw juice daily. (Always keep fruit and vegetable juices separate; this will provide an effective, specific healing process and avoid bloating or heartburn.) If you suffer from diabetes or are hypoglycaemic, drink 100 ml daily or sip slowly over a period of 1 hour so as not to throw out your blood sugar levels.

Carrot juice

Use carrot juice as a basis for all your vegetable juices. It is the elixir of all juices for cleansing, healing and regeneration of cell tissue; it is the basic juice of healing for the skin in acne, pimples, dermatitis and arthritis; it is high in beta carotene (natural vitamin A), which is one of our greatest scavengers of free radical damage of cell tissue, particularly for the cleansing and healing of the liver – the filter system of the body; and it is high in enzymes, which assist digestion.

 The effects of some vegetables can be very powerful when juiced, so you need to take care when trying new options. Sip slowly on new juices, and if you experience any abdominal pain or diarrhoea, speak to your naturopath about the juice's suitability for you.

Tomato juice

This is high in oxalic acid and can be a problem to those who suffer itchy skin, kidney stones, heartburn and any digestive problems including colitis, irritable bowel or peptic ulcer. Tomatoes are high in vitamin C and Lycopene, an essential active substance that helps prevent prostate cancer.

Cabbage juice

This is used specifically for healing peptic ulcers, but it is very strong in taste and can make you feel nauseated. Cabbage juice is best mixed with carrot juice.

Wheat grass juice

This is great for diluting free radicals and for cancer protection, but it can make you feel nauseated. Like cabbage juice, mix wheat grass juice with carrot juice or dilute with water and sip a half-glass slowly.

Garlic juice

This is high in natural sulphur, which when juiced raw and drunk with other vegetables can upset the digestion. Use 1 clove daily in juice if you would like to try it for bronchial problems.

   Broccoli, cauliflower, brussels sprouts (members of the Brassica family) are all excellent anti-oxidant vegetables but generally taste a lot better lightly steamed in salads. Asparagus is similar.

Carrot and celery

makes 250 ml

This juice eases arthritis and sore joints. Celery juice is high in natural sodium to assist joint mobility.

2½ medium carrots, trimmed and washed
1¼ sticks of celery, washed

Combine ingredients in an electric juicer, then process and serve.

Carrot and beetroot

makes 250 ml

This juice helps fight acne and dermatitis. The carrot juice detoxifies the liver; the beetroot juice cleanses the spleen, which is helpful for vibrant skin.

3½ medium carrots, trimmed and washed
1 small wedge of beetroot (approximately 25 g), washed

Combine ingredients in an electric juicer, then process and serve.

Carrot and ginger

makes 250 ml

This juice soothes constipation. The carrot juice stimulates liver enzymes and cleans a sluggish liver, stimulating cleansing of the bowel; the ginger increases circulation and brings heat and life to a slow bowel and sore joints.

4 medium carrots, trimmed and washed
small knob of fresh ginger (approximately 10 g), peeled

Combine ingredients in an electric juicer, then process and serve.

Carrot, beetroot and ginger

makes 250 ml

This juice is wonderful for those with arthritis or cold hands and feet. The ginger assists circulation to external joints; the carrot juice and beetroot juice clear the liver, allowing fewer free radicals to accumulate in joints.

3–4 medium carrots, trimmed and washed
1 small wedge of beetroot (approximately 25 g)
3 knobs ginger (approximately 30 g), peeled

Combine ingredients in an electric juicer, then process and serve.

Carrot, spinach and beet greens

makes 250 ml

This juice is ideal for anaemia sufferers and for women as a pep-up before periods. The spinach contains high amounts of chlorophyll, folic acid and iron. For women who do not absorb iron well, drink this juice daily or until your iron levels are normal, then drink it twice a week.

1½ medium carrots, trimmed and washed
½ bunch English spinach, washed
5–6 beetroot stems and leaves, washed

Combine ingredients in an electric juicer, then process and serve.

Carrot, celery and parsley

makes 250 ml

This juice eases fluid retention. Celery is a wonderful, safe diuretic, particularly for fluid retention associated with diseases and also before a woman's period. Parsley is a strong herb and is high in folic acid; use a little, because it can be a powerful cleanser of the kidneys.

2 large carrots, trimmed and washed
2 sticks celery
6 sprigs parsley, washed

Combine ingredients in an electric juicer, then process and serve.

Carrot, cabbage and turmeric

makes 250 ml

This juice is ideal for people with ulcers, an irritable bowel, cancer or varicose veins. The cabbage juice contains an amazing vitamin called vitamin U, which has a wonderful history of healing all forms of ulcers and inflamed mucus membranes. (Research is continuing regarding the benefits of cabbage as an anti-cancer agent.) Turmeric is a great anti-oxidant for heart disease, cancer, arthritis and any liver disease. This formula is an excellent way to destroy parasites in the bowel. (If you are not used to the taste of cabbage juice, sip on this formula slowly so your digestion can adapt to its concentration. Add 1 clove of garlic for added antibacterial effect, especially useful to fight against parasites in the bowel.)

1½ medium carrots, trimmed and washed
⅛ of medium cabbage (approximately 285 g), washed and shredded
1 knob fresh turmeric (or ½ teaspoon powder)

Combine ingredients in an electric juicer, then process and serve.

❦ Raw fruit juices

Drink raw fruit juices daily for their high content of enzymes, vitamin C, anti-oxidants and for a general sugar boost. It is best to drink them an hour before or after food, for complete digestion.

I recommend 1 large glass (approximately 250 ml) of raw juice daily. If you have diabetes or hypoglycaemia do not use concentrated fruit juices; instead see your naturopath. You may wish to either sip on these juices slowly (only 100 ml per day) or dilute them with water: 100 ml juice and 100 ml water.

Just as carrot juice is the ideal base for vegetable juices, you can use orange juice or apple juice as a base for fruit juices in the citrus family. And remember, for an effective, specific healing process and to avoid bloating or heartburn, do not mix fruit juices with vegetable juices. I also always recommend keeping citrus fruits separate; stone fruits by themselves; and fruits with little seed separate. It is better for your digestion, particularly if you suffer from allergies.

Orange and lemon

makes 250 ml

This juice fights colds, flus and bronchial problems. All orange fruits (and vegetables) are high in anti-oxidants, which work against a sluggish liver and major diseases such as cancer and cardiovascular disease. Orange juice is very high in vitamin C; the whole pith put back in the juice holds the bioflavonoids, which are a natural anti-inflammatory for sinus passages. Lemon juice is great at cleaning the body of mucus, and it also stimulates the digestive juices, particularly in the liver and pancreas.

If you are very 'fluey', add 1 teaspoon chopped fresh ginger to this juice. If this upsets your digestion (mixing a vegetable with fruit, see the note on page 36), alternate slow sips of this juice with a glass of water with honey. This last option is excellent if you have a flu-related fever.

2½ medium oranges, peeled leaving a little of the pith, chopped and seeds removed
1 small lemon, peeled leaving a little of the pith, chopped and seeds removed

Combine ingredients in an electric juicer, then process and serve.

Orange, pineapple, lemon and grapefruit

makes 250 ml

This juice eases sinus problems and arthritis. Although an acidic fruit, pineapple contains high amounts of a bioflavonoid called bromelain, which can assist joint pain and soothe inflamed sinus passages. The orange juice assists the liver.

½ medium orange, peeled leaving a little of the pith, chopped and seeds removed
200 g pineapple, skin removed and cored
½ small lemon, peeled leaving a little of the pith, chopped and seeds removed
½ medium grapefruit, peeled leaving a little of the pith, chopped and seeds removed

Combine ingredients in an electric juicer, then process and serve.

Muscat grape

makes 250 ml

This is a great blood cleanser and is excellent as part of a detox program. Although high in sugar, muscat grapes are also high in flavonoids (anti-oxidants that fight against cancer) and vitamin C. Dilute the juice with water (50 per cent juice, 50 per cent water) if you have hypoglycaemia. This juice is wonderful for children who are anaemic or do not like eating green vegetables.

2–3 cups of muscat grapes, washed and stems removed

Place grapes in an electric juicer, then process and serve.

Peach, apricot and mango

makes 250 ml

This juice provides an anti-oxidant liver boost for the skin and aids digestion. All these fruits are from the 'stone' family and agree with digestion. They are high in the 'orange' colour flavonoids called caratoids that scavenge free radicals in the body, particularly in the liver. This juice is wonderful for those who need a very alkaline effect on the blood, or who suffer from heartburn, an irritable bowel or acne.

175 g peaches, stones removed
200 g apricots, stones removed
200 g firm mango, peeled and stone removed

Combine ingredients in an electric juicer, then process and serve.

Strawberry, kiwifruit and white grape

makes 250 ml

This juice enhances the immune system to fight bronchitis, flus and colds. These 'little seed' fruits can be acidic to those with sensitive skin, but they are very high in vitamin C. Drink 1 glass a day before the winter months (at least 3 weeks before).

⅓ cup (approximately 100 g) strawberries, stems removed and washed
⅓ cup (approximately 100 g) kiwifruit, peeled
1 cup white grapes, washed and stems removed

Combine ingredients in an electric juicer, then process and serve.

Cherry

makes 250 ml

This juice targets anaemia, gout, arthritis and rheumatism. It is a wonderful fruit for a rich supply of iron for anaemia and joint pain; cherries clear out the spleen (storage of blood cells) and assist the pancreas (controls sugar levels in blood). You can mix this juice with dark grape juice for children who suffer from anaemia, because the grape juice makes the juice sweeter and adds more anti-oxidants for growth and good health.

5 cups pitted fresh cherries, washed

Place cherries in an electric juicer, then process and serve.

Apple

makes 250 ml

This juice is beneficial for cigarette smokers and those with indigestion, choles-terol, toxic exposure to lead and mercury, and cancer. Apples contain pectin, an active ingredient that clears fat from arteries and helps eliminate from the liver mercury from lead exposure, plus alleviate free radical damage from chemo- and radiation therapy in cancer patients.

3 medium apples

Place apples in an electric juicer, then process and serve.

Mulberry, blackberry, raspberry and cranberry

makes 250 ml

This juice targets cystitis, kidney problems, a sluggish liver, incontinence and prostate cancer. Filled with anti-oxidants, it is powerful against major diseases, but it can be very sweet, so add water if necessary. This juice is excellent for eld-erly people who have a weak bladder. Berries are also thought to assist vision. If you are unable to find the fresh berries, buy small bottles of organic juice and mix in the same proportions as the recipe.

approximately 1 cup mulberries
approximately 1 cup blackberries

½ cup raspberries
1 cup cranberries

Combine ingredients in an electric juicer, then process and serve.

Pear

makes 250 ml

This juice soothes constipation, an irritable bowel, coughs and sinus pain. It is gentle as a laxative for irregular bowel motions, and is safe for all ages over three years.

3 medium, firm ripe pears

Place pears in an electric juicer, then process and serve.

Watermelon

makes 250 ml

This juice alleviates fluid retention, an irritable bowel and depression. It is a wonderful juice for all ages, and cools the body in summer. You can juice the white rind, which is high in silicon to assist skin, nails and hair. Watermelon juice is also a great diuretic to prevent fluid retention for women before periods.

approximately 400 g watermelon flesh, seeds removed
approximately 10 g watermelon rind

Combine ingredients in an electric juicer, then process and serve.

Herbal teas

Herbal teas can play a vital, nourishing role in preventing and treating ailments. As a herbalist and naturopath, I have created a range of organic loose-leaf teas that will help you increase your daily fluid intake as well as prevent and soothe common ailments affecting the digestive and nervous systems. These teas also help carry nutrients around the body and stimulate the excretion of wastes from the blood.

Herbal teas can be used in a number of ways: as a warm tea drink all year round or as iced tea (or even in iceblock form) in summer. Herbal teas are also a great substitute for fizzy drinks filled with sugar, preservatives and colourings; and you can add honey to sweeten all herbal teas if you or your children have a sweet tooth.

Only buy organic herbal tea in the organic loose-leaf form. The tea in herbal tea bags is generally ground down to a powder and has therefore lost the essential oil that is needed in the healing effect of the tea. They may have a nice taste through added flavourings, but they will not have the therapeutic value required.

All of my herbal teas are organic loose-leaf with ingredients grown in Australia. Use the following guide to assist your choice.

※ **Apres** contains chamomile, fennel, aniseed and peppermint. This tea is suitable for those who suffer anxiety, stress, poor digestion, heartburn and mild insomnia. Fennel, aniseed and peppermint all benefit those with poor digestion and help calm an aggravated stomach.

※ **Berry** contains hawthorn berries, elder berries and juniper berries. Hawthorn berry assists circulatory problems and has anti-oxidant properties. Elder and juniper berries assist the sweet taste of this natural herbal tea.

※ **Chamomile tea** is excellent for colic, PMS, digestive pain and insomnia.

※ **Green tea** contains some caffeine but also has polyphenols, which are a great anti-oxidant for the lungs and liver.

※ **Lemon Tang** contains lemongrass and peppermint. This tea is ideal after fatty meals to help in the digestive process. It is cooling and soothing in hot weather and assists with kidney function.

※ **Peppermint tea** aids digestion, especially after fatty food, fish and meat dishes.

※ **Petal** contains organic red clover, lemongrass, lavender, rose petals and chamomile. This tea assists in cleaning the blood. Red clover has been used throughout history as a blood purifier. Lavender, chamomile and rose petals are known to be calmative plants, relaxing and healing for those who suffer stress and anxiety.

※ **Summer delight** contains organic spearmint, peppermint, lemongrass and aniseed. This minty tea is ideal for assisting digestion by stimulating digestive enzymes and relaxing and calming the body. Peppermint has a long history of aiding digestion of fish and meat dishes.

※ **Triple E** contains liquorice root, aniseed, fennel and peppermint. This tea has a profound healing effect on the bowel and stomach, helping with sluggishness and heartburn. Pure liquorice root works as a mild anti-inflammatory, hence liquorice is used in most cough medicine and laxative-type medication.

Breakfasts

Fruit salads

For good digestion and to avoid bloating and reflux, it is always best to make a fruit salad with the ideal groups of fruits.

Citrus fruit salad
pineapple

oranges

mandarins

grapefruit

Stone fruit salad
mangoes

peaches

nectarines

Cut all the fruit into cubes and mix in a large bowl. Sprinkle with a little raw sugar or a drizzle of honey.

If you have a strong digestive system you can mix together any fruits you love, and then add the pulp of 2 passionfruit or a sprinkle of raw sugar and the juice of 1 orange.

Buckwheat pancakes

makes approximately 16 pancakes

Buckwheat is a gluten-free 'energy' grain containing high amounts of a bioflavo-noid called 'rutin', which helps strengthen blood vessels, especially with varicose veins and broken capillaries. Buckwheat is high in vitamins B1 and B6, niacin, folic acid and potassium. These pancakes are a great nutritious breakfast for the entire family, with your favourite fresh fruit or protein on top.

1 cup buckwheat flour

1 cup water (you can use milk instead of water for a thicker consistency)

1 tablespoon ground arrowroot

1 tablespoon light vegetable oil

¼ cup light olive oil for frying

In a bowl combine the flour, water, arrowroot and vegetable oil. Whisk the mixture until it is smooth and free of lumps.

Place a small frying pan over high heat and then add a little olive oil. Using a small ladle, pour in a small amount of the pancake mixture, approximately 1 tablespoon. Cook for 30 seconds or until small bubbles form in the mixture, then flip the pancake over and repeat on the second side until the pancake is brown all over. Drain the pancake on paper towel to remove any excess oil. Add more oil when necessary and cook until all the batter is used.

Oat porridge (the old-fashioned way)

serves 3–4

Oats are the number-one grain for the nervous system and for restoring energy when you are run-down and stressed. They also lower cholesterol, strengthen heart muscles and raise the body temperature (ideal in cold weather). Eat oats daily for energy in high-stress situations such as sport and work.

Oats are very high in silicon (a mineral that helps bones and connective tissue) and phosphorus (a mineral that aids concentration; ideal for children), and they are also a great anti-ageing grain.

1 cup whole organic rolled oats   ½ teaspoon sea salt
5 cups water

In a saucepan combine the oats, water and salt. Soak overnight if you have the time. Bring to the boil and then reduce heat and simmer for 1–2 hours. The longer the oats simmer, the more delicious they become. Alternatively, you can cook the oats overnight in a rice cooker.

Serve with fruit, milk, raisins or prunes.

Wholemeal pancakes

makes 10 pancakes

This is a perfect luncheon dish served with a mixed green salad or Caesar salad (see page 66), or see the delicious fillings listed opposite.

1 cup wholemeal or light white flour	pinch of sea salt
1 free-range egg	¼ cup soda water
1 cup skim milk	¼ cup olive oil, for frying

In the bowl of an electric mixer combine the flour, egg, milk and salt. Mix well until the mixture is very smooth; it should be slightly thick but a little runny. Transfer the mixture to a bowl and refrigerate for at least 1 hour.

Remove the mixture from the refrigerator and add the soda water. Stir the mixture gently as it froths a little.

Place a small frying pan over high heat and then add a little oil. Using a small ladle, pour in a small amount of the pancake mixture. Cook for 30 seconds or until small bubbles form in the mixture, then flip the pancake over and repeat on the second side until the pancake is brown all over. Drain the pancake on paper towel to remove any excess oil.

Try the following suggested fillings (these are especially good if you want to serve the pancakes at a party).

※ Chopped smoked salmon or trout with dill and finely chopped cucumber

※ Mushrooms sautéed with onions and garlic, with 1 teaspoon of light sour cream and seasoned with salt and pepper

※ Finely chopped ham blended with pickled cucumber (you can add a little low-fat mayonnaise to help blend the mix)

※ Finely chopped smoked salmon, dill and crème fraîche, with a little light sour cream and salmon roe caviar on top of the rolled pancake

Oatmeal porridge (the faster way)

serves 3–4

1 cup organic rolled oats   2½–3 cups cold water

In a saucepan combine the oats and water. Cook, stirring, over a low heat for 5–8 minutes or until the mixture has thickened.

Homemade muesli

serves 4–5

Using unprocessed organic ingredients, and filled with natural fibre and vita-mins B and E, muesli is a brilliant start to the day. Lecithin contains choline and inositol, which lower fats and cholesterol. Inositol is also vital in nerve functions.

½ cup wheatgerm

½ cup organic whole organic oats

¼ cup lecithin

½ cup sultanas

¼ cup raisins

½ cup slivered almonds

¼ teaspoon ground cinnamon (optional)

½ cup finely chopped dried apples or apricots (optional)

In a bowl combine all the ingredients. Mix well, then serve with yoghurt, milk, rice or soy milk. Add cinnamon or dried fruit for extra flavour, if desired.

Store leftovers in an airtight container in the refrigerator.

Energy porridge – a travelling breakfast

serves 1

Prepare this at night and store in a thermos until morning. I used this recipe every day when I was studying (I always enjoyed it with goat's milk and honey), so I highly recommend it for students, and for sportspeople.

1 tablespoon cracked organic wheat

½ tablespoon buckwheat

½ tablespoon organic rolled oats

boiling water

In a thermos combine the wheat, buckwheat and oats. Pour boiling water over the grains to cover by at least 3 cm and tighten the lid.

In the morning, serve the porridge with honey and milk either at home, at the office, or after your early-morning exercise.

Scrambled curried eggs

serves 2

This is a nutritious, exotic way to serve eggs. Eggs are a complete protein and high in lecithin and choline. The yolk contains some cholesterol, but two eggs every second day for those who have normal cholesterol levels is suitable.

1 tablespoon vegetable oil

1 onion, finely chopped

1 handful fresh curry leaves, torn

1 green chilli, finely chopped

4 free-range eggs, beaten

Heat the oil in a frying pan, add the onion and cook until it is brown. Add the curry leaves, chilli and the beaten eggs and cook, stirring, for 1 minute or until the eggs are soft and light.

Remove curry leaves and serve eggs with toast or fresh yoghurt.

The healthy omelette

serves 1

This is a great way to use eggs as a healthy protein or a light meal.

Omelette

2 free-range eggs (if you have high
    cholesterol, use only the egg whites)

1 tablespoon water or low-fat milk

olive oil

Vegetarian filling 1

1 tomato, finely chopped

1 onion, finely chopped

4 fresh basil leaves

Vegetarian filling 2

1 medium mushroom, finely sliced

1 small carrot, finely chopped

1 small stick celery, finely sliced

1 leaf English spinach, washed
    and finely chopped

Meat filling

1–2 slices of your favourite cooked
    cold meats, such as turkey, chicken
    or lamb, finely chopped

Cheese filling

1 tablespoon low-fat cottage cheese
    or 2–3 thin slices mozzarella

In a bowl whisk the eggs with the water or milk.

Add a little oil to a frying pan over medium heat. Pour in the egg mixture, reduce heat to low and cook the omelette until the edge is curling a little; use a spatula to gently lift the edge of the omelette and check that it is slightly brown underneath. Add your favourite filling to one half of the omelette, then flip the other half over the top. Cook for 1 minute or until heated through, and serve.

Salads and dressings

Carrot and sultana salad

serves 2

Children love this because it is sweet, and it encourages them to eat carrots, which are high in anti-oxidants and enzymes. You can add some honey to this salad for children who love extra sweetening. Children also love this with boiled eggs (a protein that contains lecithin, an important vitamin that assists certain brain pathways and development).

3 carrots, grated
juice of 1 orange

1 cup dried currants or sultanas
2 tablespoons desiccated coconut (optional)

In a salad bowl combine all the ingredients. Toss well and serve.

Rice salad

serves 4

This is a great salad to serve for lunch with a protein such as tuna, chicken or beans on the side or tossed through at the last minute. You can prepare this to take to work, with the protein in a separate container.

3 cups cooked brown rice, cooled (see page 93)

1 cup cooked peas

¼ cup deseeded and finely chopped red or green capsicum

2 tablespoons finely chopped fresh parsley

1 tablespoon toasted sesame seeds

2 tablespoons currants

2 tablespoons finely chopped chives (or shallots)

¼ cup Healthy French Dressing (see page 70)

½ teaspoon ground turmeric

1 teaspoon ground cumin (optional)

In a large salad bowl combine the rice, peas, capsicum, parsley, sesame seeds, currants and chives. Drizzle the Healthy French Dressing over the salad and then sprinkle with the turmeric and cumin (if using) to serve.

My favourite Niçoise salad

serves 2

This is a very nutritious salad to throw together in summer when you are tired and tempted to have takeaway. Vary the ingredients as you like, but remember that the principle stays the same: use one, two or three proteins with a base of lettuce and one or two steamed vegetables. The protein can be varied to eggs, chicken or legumes such as chickpeas, lima beans or a can of mixed beans. A mix of two or three proteins gives added energy. You can change the potato to any steamed vegetable.

1 teaspoon balsamic vinegar

3 teaspoons extra-virgin olive oil

2 free-range eggs

4 baby new potatoes, steamed

½ lettuce, washed and chopped

1 × 100 g can tuna or salmon, drained

vegetable salt and freshly cracked black pepper, to taste

In a small jug combine the balsamic vinegar and oil.

Boil the eggs for 4 minutes, then remove them from the water and shell them. Set them aside to cool and then cut them in half.

Boil or steam the potatoes until just tender. (Use a sharp skewer to check.)

In a large bowl combine the egg, potato, lettuce and tuna/salmon. Mix these ingredients and then drizzle the dressing over the top. Season with vegetable salt and pepper and serve.

Jamie's lentil and bacon salad

serves 4

This recipe from my nephew Jamie Sach is a great accompaniment to barbe-cued meat, steamed fish and grilled chicken. Vegetarians can easily adapt this dish by leaving out the bacon and using vegetable stock.

3 cups brown lentils or green Puy-style lentils, soaked for several hours (overnight is ideal)

3 cups stock (see pages 75–76 for Vegetable Stock and Chicken Stock)

2 rashers bacon, fat trimmed and finely chopped

sea salt and freshly cracked black pepper, to taste

1 medium onion, finely chopped

2 sticks celery, finely chopped

1 large carrot, finely chopped

1 small bunch fresh parsley, roughly chopped

2 cloves garlic, crushed or finely chopped

2 tablespoons red-wine vinegar (balsamic will do but it is quite strong, so go easy)

2 tablespoons extra-virgin olive oil

Drain the lentils and transfer them to a saucepan with the stock and bacon. Bring to the boil, reduce heat to low and simmer, stirring occasionally, for 15–20 minutes or until the lentils only just begin to soften; the lentils cook by absorption and soak up the flavour of the stock, leaving only a little residual moisture (top with a little water

if the mixture begins to dry). Season the lentils with salt and pepper
and then put aside to cool.

Toss the onion, celery and carrot through the lentils and then
mix through the parsley. In a jug combine the garlic, red-wine vinegar
and olive oil and mix through the salad. Check seasoning and serve.

Avocado, mint and pea salad

Serves 4–6

*This is a great salad for healthy skin, to combat arthritis (apple cider vinegar is
excellent for joints) and a sluggish liver and bowel. The fresh mint assists digestion. You can use 1 drained 200 g can of green beans instead of fresh peas. Serve
the salad with a protein or a vegetarian dish, such as steamed tofu on the side or
grated cheese on top of the salad.*

200 g freshly shelled peas

3 avocados, peeled and cut into
  cubes

½ cup chopped fresh mint leaves

2 tablespoons apple cider vinegar

1 tablespoon honey

1 chilli, finely chopped (optional)

1 small onion, finely sliced

Place the peas in a saucepan and cover them with water. Place them
over heat and simmer for 15 minutes or until tender. Drain the peas
and transfer them to a large salad bowl. Add the remaining ingredients and toss well.

Mixed salad with nuts

serves 4

Rocket contains chlorophyll, which aids absorption of iron in the blood. Walnuts are high in omega 6 and excellent for lungs and poor circulation; they are delicious roasted. You can use pine nuts instead if you prefer. Tahini is made from sesame seeds, which are high in minerals and protein. If you don't like tahini, you can substitute the dressing by mixing 2 tablespoons olive oil and the juice of 1 lemon.

olive oil

1 cup walnuts, chopped, or
    ¼ cup pine nuts

1 small bunch mixed rocket and
    other salad leaves, washed
    and roughly chopped

1 small bunch watercress, leaves
    picked, washed and roughly
    chopped

2 tomatoes, cut into chunks

1 cucumber, cut into 1-cm slices

1–2 tablespoons tahini dressing

Heat a little olive oil in a frying pan and sauté the nuts for 5 minutes or until brown. Remove from heat and place on a paper towel, to drain the oil.

In a salad bowl, combine the nuts, salad leaves, watercress, tomato and cucumber, then drizzle the tahini dressing over the salad to serve.

Egg and asparagus salad

serves 2

This salad is quick, easy and nutritious for lunch or a light dinner. Eggs are a wonderful complete light protein. I often prepare this in the evening for lunch the following day. Add some boiled new potatoes for a carbohydrate, or eat with bread. You can also add other vegetables, such as steamed carrots or zucchini.

2 free-range eggs

½ bunch asparagus, washed and trimmed

2 tablespoons extra-virgin olive oil

½ teaspoon sea salt

1 medium avocado, peeled and cut into cubes

½ bunch rocket, washed and torn

¼ onion, finely chopped

Boil the eggs for 4 minutes, then drain the eggs and run under cold water for 2 minutes. Shell and cut into quarters.

Bring a saucepan of salted water to the boil. Add the asparagus and cook for 3–5 minutes or until tender. Drain the asparagus, cut into 2-cm lengths and then place in a bowl, adding the oil and salt.

In a large salad bowl combine the remaining ingredients. Add the egg and asparagus and toss thoroughly to serve.

Butter bean, potato and spinach salad

serves 4

This salad is a perfect combination of protein (beans), carbohydrate (potato) and a green vegetable, with a healthy dressing. This can be a complete meal in summer or served as a side salad to a fish or chicken dish. It's great for those cutting back on meat and chicken and wanting to increase energy and keep weight down.

Salad

4 medium potatoes, peeled and quartered

4 salad onions, halved lengthways

freshly cracked black pepper, to taste

1 × 400 g can butter beans, drained

100 g baby spinach leaves, washed

2 cloves garlic, crushed

Dressing

2 tablespoons balsamic vinegar

1 tablespoon wholegrain mustard (optional)

1 tablespoon honey

2 tablespoons chopped fresh parsley

Preheat oven to 180°C.

Arrange the potato and salad onion on a baking tray. Sprinkle with pepper (use no oils) and bake until the potatoes are soft and slightly brown – about 1 hour.

While the potatoes and salad onions are baking, combine the dressing ingredients in a bowl. Mix well, then set the dressing aside.

Transfer the hot potato and salad onion to a salad bowl and add the remaining ingredients. Mix well, drizzle the dressing over and serve immediately.

Chickpea and avocado salad

serves 4

Chickpeas are a nutritious legume, and are higher in protein than eggs and many meats. Chickpeas are also high in B vitamins, calcium, iron, zinc and potassium. Avocado is rich in omega 6 oils for healthy skin and hair.

Salad

1 medium carrot, finely sliced

2 medium zucchini, finely sliced

2 cups cooked or drained canned chickpeas (about 2 × 400 g cans)

1 onion, finely chopped

½ cup black olives, chopped

2 avocados, peeled and sliced

Dressing

2 tablespoons tamari

1 clove garlic, chopped

1 tablespoon honey

juice of ½ lemon

1 tablespoon roasted slivered almonds, sesame seeds or pine nuts (optional)

In a jug combine the dressing ingredients. Mix well.

Boil or steam the carrot and zucchini slices, along with the chickpeas, for 5 minutes, then drain and transfer them to a salad bowl.

Add the remaining salad ingredients and toss gently. Drizzle the dressing over and toss before serving.

Jamie's whole sardines with roasted garlic, olive and fennel salad

serves 2

Jamie, my well-loved nephew, is a highly regarded sommelier in Adelaide, and is at present Penfolds' brand ambassador. This healthy dish is a 'hit'. Sardines are very high in omega 3 oils, essential for lowering cholesterol and for dry skin irritations and cell membrane integrity in the brain. Fennel is a natural calmative assisting digestion and 'calming' natural digestive processes.

1 head garlic

olive oil, for baking

2 cups breadcrumbs

2 tablespoons finely chopped
  fresh parsley

sea salt and freshly cracked
  black pepper, to taste

8–10 whole sardines, cleaned,
  rinsed and patted dry

1 bulb fennel, finely sliced

1 medium red onion, finely sliced

½ cup pitted black olives

1 tablespoon capers

1 tablespoon verjuice (or lemon
  juice or red-wine vinegar)

parsley leaves, to serve

2 tablespoons olive oil

1 lemon, cut into wedges

Preheat oven to 180°C.

Break up the head of garlic and roast the cloves whole with the skin on in a baking dish with a drizzle of olive oil for 15–20 minutes or until they soften. Remove the garlic from the oven (and increase oven temperature to 200°C) and set aside while you continue with the following steps.

Place the breadcrumbs in a large bowl and add the finely chopped parsley and a generous amount of salt and pepper. Stuff the cavity of the sardines with some of the breadcrumb mixture, then roll them in it to coat thoroughly.

Line the sardines in a lightly oiled baking dish and bake for 10–12 minutes (alternatively you can shallow-fry the sardines in olive oil for a crunchier texture).

Meanwhile, combine the fennel and red onion in a large bowl. Add the olives, capers, roasted garlic cloves, verjuice, some whole parsley leaves and 2 tablespoons olive oil, and season with salt and pepper. Arrange the salad on a serving plate and place the whole cooked sardines on top. Serve with wedges of lemon.

Couscous salad

serves 4

With herbs and flowers, this salad looks great in summer on the table with barbecued seafood. This light grain salad is filling, but not as heavy as brown rice. Couscous is high in vitamins, minerals and fibre, especially vitamin B1, B2 and B6, niacin, magnesium and maganese, phosphorus and potassium. It aids in stabilising blood sugar and energy levels and is useful for hypoglycaemia and hormone-related mood swings, as well as providing energy for athletes and children, especially children who are overweight. If edible flowers are unavailable, add some sprigs of fresh herbs instead.

2 cups couscous

3 cups hot water

1 tablespoon lemon juice

juice of 1 lemon

1 small bunch edible flowers, such as zucchini flowers or nasturtiums, washed (optional)

100 g roasted pine nuts, almonds or cashews, chopped

1 tablespoon chopped fresh coriander or parsley

¼ cup chopped fresh mint

1 cup dried apricots, sliced

2 tablespoons finely grated lemon zest

In a large bowl combine the couscous, hot water and the tablespoon of lemon juice. Stir and set aside, covered, to soak for 10–15 minutes.

Meanwhile, place the lemon juice in a medium stainless steel mixing bowl – it should be large enough to just hold all the couscous. Press some of the edible flowers (if using) onto the base of the bowl.

When the couscous has soaked up the water, add the nuts, coriander or parsley, mint, apricot and lemon zest, and mix well with a fork, fluffing the couscous as you stir. Transfer the couscous to the bowl containing the lemon juice and the flowers, and press the mixture down flat and flush with the top of the bowl. Firmly hold a flat plate over the top of the bowl, invert the bowl to turn out the couscous salad with the flowers. If this sounds a little ambitious, simply serve the salad straight from the bowl – it won't look as pretty, but it will taste just as good.

Decorate the salad with the remaining flowers and refrigerate until ready to serve.

My favourite Caesar salad

serves 4

This salad should be served with a simple protein such as grilled fish, chicken or meat, or a legume dish. Both tasty and gentle on the digestion, this salad is a hit for entertaining at home.

1 iceberg lettuce, outer leaves removed and lettuce washed and dried in a colander

3 hardboiled free-range eggs, quartered

4 slices prosciutto

½ teaspoon chopped fresh oregano

olive oil, for frying

2 tablespoons shaved parmesan

freshly cracked black pepper

1 handful chopped fresh parsley

Croutons (or use ½ packet ready-made croutons)

2 cloves garlic, finely chopped

½ teaspoon paprika

½ cup olive oil

6 slices bread, cut into cubes (crusts removed)

Dressing

¼ cup balsamic vinegar or white-wine vinegar

½ cup extra-virgin olive oil

1 teaspoon Dijon mustard

juice of ½ lemon

3–4 anchovy fillets

sea salt and freshly cracked black pepper, to taste

To make the croutons, heat the oil in a frying pan for 30 seconds and then add the garlic and paprika. Add the bread cubes and mix until the cubes are well coated. Transfer to a microwave-proof dish. Micro-wave for 3–5 minutes (or you can bake them on an oven tray at 180°C for 15 minutes) until the cubes are lightly browned. Set aside.

In a blender mix the vinegar, olive oil, mustard, lemon juice and anchovies until the mixture is thick but runny. Season with salt and pepper to taste and set the dressing aside while you prepare the salad.

Tear the lettuce leaves into pieces and place in a salad bowl. Add the eggs to the bowl.

Add a little oil to a frying pan and place over medium heat. Add the prosciutto slices and then sprinkle with the oregano. Cook for 5 minutes or until crispy, then remove the prosciutto and allow it to cool a little. When it has cooled, break it into chunky pieces and then add to the salad bowl.

Pour the dressing over the salad and then scatter the parmesan over the top. Sprinkle with black pepper, parsley and croutons and toss gently before serving.

Beetroot and asparagus salad

serves 4

Beetroot helps cleanse the spleen, liver and pancreas. Asparagus contains aspar-agine, which eliminates excess water through the kidneys. It is also high in vitamin A (for those with lung problems) and potassium (for arthritis sufferers).

1 bunch (approximately 400 g) fresh beetroot, washed

2 bunches asparagus, washed and trimmed

1 tablespoon balsamic vinegar or lemon juice

1 red capsicum, deseeded and thinly sliced

1 tablespoon chopped fresh chives

1 tablespoon sesame seeds, toasted

Steam or boil the beetroot for 1 hour or until tender (cooking time will depend on the size of the beetroot). Remove from water – the skin will become loose – and use a knife to help you peel off the skin. Set the beetroot aside to cool slightly, then cut it into slices or cubes and transfer them to a salad bowl.

Steam or boil the asparagus for 5 minutes, then rinse under cold water. Transfer to the salad bowl with the beetroot and combine.

Drizzle the balsamic vinegar or lemon juice over the beetroot and asparagus, and mix in the capsicum. Sprinkle the chives and sesame seeds over the top and serve.

Beetroot and asparagus are used widely in cancer clinics for their nutritional properties and healing effects in eliminating free radicals from the body. This salad is a must as a preventative for disease, as well as for those with joint, liver, lung or spleen problems.

Salad dressings

You can make any salad even more delicious if you choose fresh, healthy ingredients to include in the dressing.

Try apple cider vinegar, fresh lemon juice and lime juice mixed with any cold-pressed oil you love.

Paw Paw dressing

makes 1 cup

2 cups peeled, seeded and chopped paw paw or papaya

2 tablespoons lemon juice

With an electric mixer, blend all the ingredients and serve immediately.

Healthy French dressing

makes about 2 cups

1 cup extra-virgin olive oil

¼ cup freshly squeezed lemon
  juice

½ cup apple cider vinegar

1 clove garlic, crushed (optional)

2 teaspoons honey

freshly cracked black pepper,
  to taste (optional)

With an electric mixer, blend all the ingredients. Store the dressing in
an airtight container in the refrigerator for up to 2 days.

French tomato dressing

makes 1 cup

1 cup tomato juice (or Simple
  Tomato Sauce, see page 91)

1 tablespoon lemon juice

2 tablespoons chopped fresh basil

With an electric mixer, blend all the ingredients. Store the dressing in
an airtight container in the refrigerator for up to 2 days.

Soups and stocks

Barley soup

serves 4

Barley helps increase energy and supplies nourishment for active people who need a carbohydrate and vegetable boost.

1 tablespoon olive oil

¼ onion, chopped

4 carrots, grated

2 parsnips, peeled and chopped

2 litres water

1 cup pearl barley

⅓ teaspoon grated ginger (optional)

sea salt, to taste

½ bunch fresh parsley, chopped

Heat the oil in a saucepan over medium heat. Add the onion, carrot and parsnip, and sauté for 5 minutes or until tender. Add the water, barley and ginger, then reduce heat and simmer for 1½ hours, stirring occasionally. Season with salt and add the parsley to serve.

Minestrone soup

serves 6

This nutritious soup may be portioned and frozen so you can eat it anytime or use as a snack when you arrive home late. It's great with crusty bread.

1 kg chuck steak and/or ½ free-range chicken

1 teaspoon sea salt

2 medium onions, chopped

3 cloves garlic, chopped

3 medium potatoes, peeled and chopped

3 large carrots, chopped

4 sticks celery, chopped

1 handful peas

1 handful green beans, chopped

3 large tomatoes, chopped

1 × 200 g can bean mix, drained

1 bunch English spinach, washed and chopped (optional)

200 g lentils

½ head broccoli or cauliflower, chopped

4 slices bread

2 tablespoons grated parmesan

sea salt, extra, and freshly cracked black pepper, to taste

Fill a large saucepan with 4–5 litres of water and add the chuck steak and chicken. Bring to the boil and boil for at least 2 hours to create your own broth.

Add the salt, then reduce heat to a simmer and transfer the chuck steak and chicken to a chopping board, leaving the saucepan on the stove. Remove the skin from the chicken. Cut the chuck steak and chicken into cubes and return them to the saucepan. Add the onion, garlic, potato, carrot, celery, peas, beans, tomato, bean mix, spinach, lentils, broccoli or cauliflower. Simmer for 2 hours.

When the soup is ready, toast the bread and then cut it into cubes. Sprinkle the cheese over the bread and grill for 1–2 minutes or until the cheese browns.

Season the soup with salt and pepper and serve with the cheesy croutons.

Cleansing noodle soup

serves 2

This is excellent during a detox; alternate this with the minestrone soup opposite.

1 litre Vegetable Stock (see page 75)
1 carrot, chopped
1 spring onion, chopped

2 cups dried noodles (of your choice)
1 small bunch bok choy or ½ bunch spinach (or a mix of both), washed and chopped

In a large saucepan combine the stock, carrot and onion. Place over a high heat and bring to a boil. Add the noodles, reduce heat to low, and simmer until the noodles are cooked. Add the greens and cook until they are tender then serve.

Cauliflower and broccoli soup

serves 6

My friend Suzie serves this soup at some of her wonderful parties. Cauliflower and broccoli contain anti-oxidants. They should always be cooked, because if eaten raw on a regular basis they can damage cell tissue. This hearty soup is ideal for an entrée for dinner parties as well as served in winter with chunks of hot wholemeal bread.

2 tablespoons butter

1 large head of cauliflower, finely chopped

1 large head of broccoli, finely chopped

1 bunch spring onions, chopped

1 teaspoon rock salt and 1 large pinch ground white pepper

2 pinches cayenne pepper (optional)

2 litres Vegetable or Chicken Stock (see pages 75–76)

2 free-range egg yolks

¼ cup light cream

4 sprigs fresh parsley and ½ bunch fresh chives, finely chopped and combined

½ cup yoghurt, to serve

In a large saucepan, melt the butter over medium heat. Add the cauliflower, broccoli and spring onion and stir constantly for 5–8 minutes or until the vegetables are soft. Season with salt and pepper. (Add the cayenne pepper if you like a little spice.) Add the stock and simmer for 40 minutes.

Allow the soup to cool a little, then transfer to a blender. Puree the soup, then transfer back to a large saucepan and reheat.

As the soup is heating, beat the egg yolks with the cream in a bowl. Add this mixture to the hot soup very slowly, whisking constantly to ensure the eggs do not become scrambled. Garnish with the chive–parsley mixture and yoghurt, and serve.

Vegetable, fish and chicken stocks

Homemade stocks are nutritious and far superior to commercial stocks. Use however much you need for a recipe at the time and then freeze the rest in containers.

Vegetable stock

makes about 3 litres

Kombu (seaweed), found in your health food store, is part of the kelp family and is great in soups, casseroles, salads and sautés. It assists digestion.

2 medium onions, quartered

2 large carrots, chopped

4–5 sticks celery, chopped

1 leek, washed and chopped

6-cm piece kombu (for extra flavour)

4 litres water

In a large saucepan combine all the ingredients and place over low heat. Simmer for 45 minutes. Strain, remove the kombu and throw the vegetables on the compost heap. Freeze the stock in airtight containers for future use.

Fish stock

makes about 3 litres

2 large fish heads or 1 kg prawn
  shells and heads

1 bunch fresh parsley, roughly chopped

2 large onions, chopped

3 cloves garlic, chopped

2 tablespoons fish sauce

6-cm piece kombu (optional)

4 litres water

In a large saucepan combine all the ingredients and bring to the boil,
then reduce heat and simmer for 30–40 minutes. Strain the stock and
discard all the solids (you may need to use a fine sieve). Skim any fat
from the surface. Freeze the stock in airtight containers for future use.

Chicken stock

makes about 3 litres

1 medium-size free-range chicken,
  washed

2 medium onions, roughly chopped

2 large carrots, chopped

1 medium leek, washed and chopped

3–4 sticks celery, chopped

4 litres water

In a large saucepan combine all the ingredients and bring to the boil,
then reduce heat and simmer for 1½–2 hours. Strain the stock and
cool in the refrigerator. Remove any fat from the surface. Freeze the
stock in airtight containers for future use. Use the chicken in sandwiches, soups or a risotto.

Snacks, sandwiches and side dishes

Healthy snacks for 21st-century living have become rare. Unfortunately, sugar-loaded health bars have replaced simple, quick and healthy home-cooked snacks.

People with low blood sugar levels (hypoglycaemia) need healthy snacks every 3–4 hours. Growing active children, sportspeople, students and those who work in high-pressure industries requiring 'brain energy' also need to snack.

Try the recipes in this section or some of the following quick options.

Savoury snacks

※ A handful of almonds, cashews or macadamias with a handful of raisins

※ Vita wheat or Ryvita biscuits with a slice of chicken, ham, beef

(plus a slither of wholegrain mustard) and a slice of tomato
with black pepper, or a small can of tuna or salmon
* A bowl of vegetable soup
* A toasted sandwich on wholemeal grainy bread
* 1–2 boiled eggs
* A sushi roll and miso soup

Sweet snacks

* 2 pieces of fresh fruit
* Yoghurt with honey or fruit
* A slice of wholemeal bread topped with tahini paste
  (see page 80) and honey
* A wholemeal muffin
* A slice of wholemeal cake
* Poached fruit and yoghurt
* A fruit, milk and yoghurt smoothie (you can add
  1 tablespoon whey powder for extra energy)
* A good-quality muesli bar (your health store can
  make a recommendation)

If you are watching your waistline, stay with protein snacks and
fresh fruits, not cakes, biscuits or candy.

Chickpea spread

makes about 2 cups

Chickpeas are a superb complete protein and are at their best as a spread or used in soups and casseroles. Children love chickpeas when they are made into a dip with garlic and onions, which have an antibacterial effect against colds and flus in winter. This spread is wonderful served on whole wheat bread, Lebanese bread or Vegetable Rissoles (see page 116), or as a dip with raw vegetables. You need to soak the chickpeas overnight.

2 cups chickpeas, soaked
 overnight in water (or you can
 use 2 × 400 g cans chickpeas)

½ cup lemon juice

1 tablespoon ground cumin or
 coriander

2 cloves garlic, crushed

1 medium onion, chopped

¼ cup water or apple juice

1–2 tablespoons Tahini (optional;
 see page 80)

Rinse the chickpeas and, if they are not soft, then simmer for 10 minutes. Combine all the ingredients in an electric blender. Blend until you have a smooth paste, then cover and store in the refrigerator for up to 2 weeks.

Tahini (sesame seed butter)

makes about ½ cup

You can soak sesame seeds overnight and lightly pan-roast them before grinding if you need to sprinkle them over salad. Sesame seeds are high in calcium, phosphorus and potassium, which is great for vegetarians.

1 cup sesame seeds   2 teaspoons linseed oil

Combine the sesame seeds and oil in the bowl of an electric food processor. Blend the ingredients into a paste, then cover and place in the refrigerator. This will keep, covered in the refrigerator, for up to 10 days.

Sesame seed oil is delicious for taste in any dish or used to sauté vegetables.

Avocado dip

makes about 2 cups

Avocado contains omega 6 oils, which are excellent for dry skin. Children enjoy this served with wholemeal bread, water biscuits or slices of raw carrot, celery and cucumber as an alternative to sweets and lollies after school.

2 large ripe avocados, peeled
   and chopped

2 tomatoes, finely chopped

¼ teaspoon vegetable salt

2 tablespoons lemon or lime juice

1 clove garlic, crushed (optional)

pinch of chilli (optional)

Place avocado in a bowl and mash with a fork until smooth. Add the remaining ingredients and mix well.

Jacket potato

serves 1

The potato is a wonderful form of carbohydrate. Just beneath the potato's skin is a rich variety of minerals (especially potassium, magnesium and phosphorus), so eating a potato in its jacket with fillings on top is a balanced and healthy snack. Alternatively, you can add this vegetable to any dish. Teenagers and children love jacket potatoes, and they are far superior to French fries.

1 potato per person   sea salt
dob of butter

Preheat oven to 180°C.

Wash the skin of the potato and then place the potato on a lined baking tray. Bake for 45 minutes or until the potato is soft in the centre (pierce with a skewer to test). Alternatively, cook the potato in a microwave oven for approximately 5 minutes. (The time will depend on the size of the potato.)

Transfer the potato to a serving plate. Slice the potato open or cut the top off and add a dob of butter and a sprinkle of salt, followed by your favourite topping.

Creative toppings

You can scoop out the hot potato flesh, combine it with one of the
following mixtures, pile it back into its jacket and briefly return to
the oven to warm through.

※ Finely chop 1 onion and mix with a small can of tuna or salmon,
  a little extra-virgin olive oil and sea salt.
※ Finely chop 1 tomato and mix with a touch of chilli or 1 finely
  chopped clove of garlic.

Or try the following combinations.

※ Creamed cheese and chopped chives.
※ Grated tasty cheese, melted under the grill (perfect for hungry
  teenagers).
※ Snipped fresh chives and a dob of sour cream.

Tasty sandwiches with Lavash or Lebanese bread

These sandwiches are low in carbohydrate and are excellent for those on a yeast-free diet, as well as anyone trying to lose weight, or who suffers from bloating. These sandwiches also appeal to children who are bored with standard sandwiches, especially if you slice them into 2–3 inch rolls.

Suggested fillings

Meat

chicken or ham slices

wholegrain or Dijon mustard, or
   low-fat mayonnaise

lettuce or rocket

Vegetarian

hummus

grated carrot

lettuce

Lentils

cold cooked red lentils

grated carrot

chopped capsicum

Tuna

well-drained tuna

sliced onion

grated carrot

Arrange your chosen fillings on one side of a piece of Lavash or Lebanese bread and roll, then cut into 2–3-inch strips. Do not use fillings that go soggy – such as beetroot and tomato – if you are filling a lunchbox with sandwiches that will be eaten in several hours' time.

Potato and sweet potato wedges

serves 2

This is a great carbohydrate snack to fill up on. Combined with a protein dip such as chickpea spread or avocado dip, it becomes a great snack for the family, especially children when they get home from school or even for a teenager's party. I do not recommend this dish for diabetics, however, because sweet potatoes are high in natural sugars.

2 large potatoes, washed and cut into long wedges (leave skins on)

1 large sweet potato, peeled and cut into wedges

2 tablespoons extra-virgin olive oil, for baking

sea salt and freshly cracked black pepper, to taste

Preheat oven to 180°C.

Line a baking tray with baking paper.

Dry the wedges with paper towel, then toss them in a large bowl with oil and season with salt and pepper and spread the wedges out on the baking tray. Bake for 1 hour or until the wedges are crisp on the outside.

Sprinkle some salt over the wedges and serve them with your favourite dip.

For something different, spread a little wholegrain mustard over the wedges, or coat them with mixed herbs such as dried oregano or paprika before cooking.

Cheese, tomato and basil pizza

makes 4 small pizzas

A fresh homemade pizza is a great option for the family on a weekend. Tomatoes are high in lycopene, an active constituent found to be an important nutrient for the prostate gland in men. Well-ripened tomatoes, although acidic, will alkalize the blood after digestion, therefore helping ease rheumatism. Large amounts of tomato upset calcium metabolism, so use sparingly if you suffer from arthritis or kidney stones.

Pizza base

2 cups pizza flour

1 cup warm water

1 cube fresh yeast (you will find this in your health store)

2 tablespoons olive oil

pinch of sea salt

Topping

1 × 400 g can chopped peeled tomatoes

1 clove garlic, crushed

1 teaspoon dried oregano

½ bunch fresh basil

pinch sea salt

mozzarella or parmesan, grated

To make the pizza base, place the flour in a large bowl and make a well in the centre. In a jug combine the water and yeast, stirring until the yeast has dissolved. Pour into the flour well, then add the oil and salt and mix with a wooden spoon until a dough forms.

Wash and dry your hands and then lightly flour your benchtop. Place the dough on the bench and knead: use the heel of your hand to knead the dough, pushing it gently away and pulling it back – it should take 5–10 minutes of kneading for the dough to become smooth and elastic. Return the dough to the bowl, cover with a tea towel and set aside in a warm place for 1–1½ hours or until the dough has doubled in size.

While the dough is rising, combine the tomatoes, garlic, oregano, basil and salt in a bowl.

Preheat oven to 200°C and grease 2 oven trays.

Roll the dough into circles and place on the trays (2 pizzas per tray) and cover each with tomato mixture, followed by the mozzarella or parmesan. Bake for 20 minutes or until the cheese has melted and the bases are crisp.

My favourite antipasto platter

serves 4

This is wonderful for parties or as a starter for dinner; it is also very nourishing and attractive. Serve with freshly cut baguettes or bread rolls on the side.

12 slices salami

16 black olives

8 slices ham

8 sundried tomatoes

2 medium bocconcini, sliced

12 fresh basil leaves

Arrange the ingredients in rows on a large flat serving platter, decorated with the basil leaves.

Potato, onion and cheese bake

serves 4

This dish is delicious served with grilled fish, fresh prawns or a simple grilled fillet steak – it's my favourite side dish in winter.

butter, for greasing casserole dish

5 large potatoes, peeled and finely sliced lengthways

3 onions, finely sliced

200 g tasty cheese, grated

sea salt and freshly cracked black pepper, to taste

1½ cups milk

1 tablespoon butter, for melting

Preheat oven to 180°C.

Grease a medium baking or casserole dish (a rectangular one works best) with a dob of butter. Cover the bottom of the dish with a layer of potato slices. Melt 1 tablespoon butter in a small saucepan over low heat, then using a brush spread a little butter evenly over the potato slices. Add a layer of onion slices and sprinkle some cheese and salt and pepper over the top. Repeat these rows until you have used all the ingredients, finishing with the cheese.

Add 2–3 dobs of butter to the top cheese layer and pour over the milk. Cover with foil and bake for 45 minutes, removing the foil in the last 10 minutes so the cheese browns. Serve immediately.

Buckwheat

serves 2–4

Buckwheat is a wonder energy grain with a delicious sweet and nutty flavour, but it is unfortunately highly overlooked in Western society. It is gluten-free and contains a bioflavonoid called rutin, which strengthens capillaries, blood vessels and is now claimed to be highly beneficial as an antidote to radiation. Buckwheat is an important grain for those with cardiovascular diseases, varicose veins, poor circulation, diabetes and intolerances to wheat and gluten. Try to use it 2–3 times a week. You can also try Japanese soba noodles, which are made from buckwheat flour.

If you haven't tried buckwheat before, the tastiest option is kasha, a toasted reddish-brown buckwheat you can buy from health stores. Kasha is one of the few grains that are alkaline, making it good for those with arthritis, ulcers, itchy skin conditions and heartburn.

2½ cups water

1 cup toasted buckwheat (kasha)

½ onion, chopped (optional)

½ teaspoon sea salt

Pour the water into a large saucepan and bring to the boil. Add the buckwheat, onion (if you would like some extra flavour) and salt, reduce heat and simmer, covered, for 10–15 minutes or until the grain is soft. Drain any excess water and then transfer the mixture to serving bowls.

To add extra flavour, try a splash of soy sauce, a dob of butter or a tablespoon of olive oil mixed through the grains.

Tasty grated onion and potato cakes

serves 2

Not only is this nutritious and tasty, children will love helping you make it. These are delicious served with fish or a meat dish.

2 potatoes, peeled and grated

2 zucchini, grated

2 carrots, grated

2 medium onions, grated

2 tablespoons extra-virgin olive oil

In a bowl combine all the vegetables and mix well. Add a little of the oil to a frying pan over medium heat. Form the mixture into small-medium flat potato cakes and sauté for 3–4 minutes on each side or until browned all over.

Couscous

serves 2

Couscous is a tiny grain made from wheat that is light and simple to prepare. High in niacin, fibre, calcium and magnesium, this grain can be used instead of pasta, brown rice or buckwheat as a base for stir-fries.

1 cup couscous

2½ cups warm water

pinch of sea salt

Place all the ingredients in a saucepan and place over low heat. Simmer for 1 minute and then let it stand, covered, for 10 minutes or until most of the water has soaked into the grain. Use a fork to gently fluff the grains until they are soft before serving.

Simple tomato sauce

serves 6 (or 4 with some leftover to freeze)

This simple sauce is wonderful with any pasta.

olive oil

1 medium onion, finely chopped

2 cloves garlic, chopped

3 × 400 g cans peeled crushed tomatoes, or 8 fresh large tomatoes, quartered

1 teaspoon brown or white sugar

½ bunch fresh basil, roughly chopped

Heat the oil in a frying pan and place over medium heat. Add the onion and garlic, and sauté until the onion is translucent and soft. Add the tomatoes and then refill one of the empty cans with water and add to the pan. Simmer for 2 minutes, then add the sugar and basil and simmer for 1 hour, stirring occasionally.

When serving you can add a little cream (1 teaspoon per person) or some finely chopped mushrooms for extra flavour.

Mashed potato

serves 4

I always tell my clients not to be afraid of mashed, steamed or boiled potatoes; the potato is a healthy carbohydrate and is very alkaline and soothing to upset stomachs, peptic ulcers and irritable bowels. Keep the skin on if possible to retain all the minerals. Mashed potatoes make the perfect carbohydrate alternative to bread, especially if you are allergic to wheat and grains.

4 medium–large potatoes,
  washed and halved

sea salt and freshly cracked
  black pepper, to taste

2 teaspoons unsalted butter

½ cup milk (optional)

Bring a large saucepan of water to the boil. Add the potatoes and boil for 10–15 minutes, or until the potatoes are soft. Drain the potatoes, reserving 1 tablespoon of the cooking water.

Transfer the potatoes to a large bowl. Add the reserved cooking water and the butter and milk (if using), and mash to a smooth consistency. Season with salt and pepper and serve. This is delicious with meat and fish.

Brown rice

serves 2

The outer shell of brown rice is high in B vitamins and therefore important in our busy lifestyles to balance stress, energy fluctuations, nervousness, depression and for natural fibre. It is excellent eaten daily for those with yeast and gluten intolerances. It must be chewed thoroughly and I always recommend a simple protein and vegetable dish on top. This recipe makes about 3 cups of cooked rice.

1 cup short-grain brown rice
  (organic is best)

3 cups cold water or Vegetable Stock
  (see page 75)

½ teaspoon sea salt

Wash and drain the rice and place it in a saucepan with the water and salt. Cover the saucepan and bring to a rapid boil, then reduce the heat and simmer for 30–45 minutes or until most of the liquid has been absorbed. Drain off any excess liquid.

Remove the lid, stir carefully and leave the mixture to rest, covered, for 5 minutes before serving.

Notes
※ For Thai dishes, use jasmine rice.
※ For Indian dishes, use basmati rice.
※ For risotto, use Arborio rice.

Sautéed potatoes

serves 3–4

These are wonderful served with chicken, lamb or steak.

12 new baby potatoes (leave skins on)
olive oil
2 cloves garlic, crushed

1 teaspoon fresh rosemary leaves
sea salt and freshly cracked
black pepper, to taste

Bring a large saucepan of water to the boil. Add the potatoes and boil for 10 minutes or until just cooked, then remove and drain. Set potatoes aside to cool.

Add the oil and garlic to a frying pan over low heat and sauté for 1 minute. Add the cooled potatoes and rosemary, season with salt and pepper and sauté for 1 minute. Serve immediately.

Main meals

Pan-fried salmon

serves 2

This simple dish is especially good for those with high cholesterol, who suffer from eczema or PMS, or need to lose weight. It is also wonderful for children's brain development. You can also use tuna or kingfish instead of salmon.

2 teaspoons rock salt
2 salmon fillets

olive oil
juice of 1 lemon

Spread the salt evenly over both sides of the salmon.

Place the oil and lemon juice in a frying pan and heat over medium heat. Add the salmon and cook on each side for 4 minutes or until cooked to your liking – most people prefer salmon a little pink in the middle.

Serve with three steamed vegetables, such as carrots, potato and broccoli (or three of your choice), for an extra anti-oxidant boost.

Angela's spinach and cheese bake

serves 4

My sister Angela makes this dish for her 9- and 11-year-old boys. It provides protein and calcium, and it encourages children to eat spinach.

butter, for sautéeing

½ cup chopped broccoli

½ cup chopped cauliflower

1 tablespoon pumpkin seeds

1 tablespoon soy sauce

2 cloves garlic, chopped

butter, for greasing casserole dish

1 bunch fresh spinach, washed and stems removed, and finely chopped

200 g tasty cheese, grated

4 potatoes, thinly sliced (leave skins on)

1 medium zucchini, thinly sliced

2 tomatoes, sliced

2 tablespoons tasty cheese, grated, extra

2 cups Vegetable Stock (see page 75)

2 tablespoons sesame seeds

Preheat oven to 180°C.

Heat a little butter in a frying pan over medium heat. Add the broccoli, cauliflower, pumpkin seeds, soy sauce and garlic, and sauté until the vegetables are just brown.

As the vegetables are cooking, grease the bottom of a casserole dish (34×25 cm; 6 cm deep). In a bowl mix the spinach with the cheese, then transfer the mixture to the casserole dish. Top with a layer of potato slices. Layer the stir-fried vegetable mixture over the potato, then arrange the zucchini and tomato slices on top and add the extra cheese. Sprinkle the sesame seeds over the top, then pour in the vegetable stock.

Bake for 40–50 minutes. Serve with a salad.

Rustic country Italian pasta

serves 4

My Italian friend Maria serves this pasta dish to hungry teenagers or when feeding a big family gathering. It is tasty, healthy and easy to prepare.

10 g dried porcini mushrooms – about 1 sachet

400 g dried spaghetti

½ cup olive oil

2 cloves garlic, sliced

1 × 185 g can tuna in oil, drained

100 g pancetta, finely chopped (optional)

1 × 400 g can diced tomatoes

Add the porcini mushrooms to a cup of warm water and leave to soak for 20 minutes.

Bring a large saucepan of salted water to the boil. Add the spaghetti and boil for 10 minutes or until al dente.

While the spaghetti is cooking, heat the oil in a frying pan over high heat. Add the garlic, drained porcini, tuna, pancetta and tomatoes, and cook, stirring, for 5 minutes.

Drain the spaghetti and divide among serving bowls. Pour the sauce over the spaghetti and serve with a salad on the side.

Maria's peasant-style chicken with rosemary

serves 4

This is a country dish from my friend Maria. It makes a great meal for all the family, especially on a cold winter evening. Rosemary is a great anti-oxidant herb for the brain. This rustic casserole is wonderful served with steamed green beans and crusty bread to mop up the juices.

4 free-range chicken Marylands

3 cloves garlic, chopped

1 onion, sliced

½ bunch fresh parsley leaves, chopped

½ bunch fresh rosemary leaves, chopped

sea salt and freshly cracked black pepper, to taste

3 medium potatoes, washed and halved

3 tablespoons extra-virgin olive oil

375 ml dry white wine

3 tablespoons grated parmesan

Preheat oven to 180°C.

Place the chicken in a medium-sized baking dish.

In a bowl combine the garlic, onion, parsley and rosemary, then sprinkle the mixture over the chicken and season with salt and pepper.

Wedge the potato halves between the chicken pieces, then drizzle oil over the top. Pour the wine over and then sprinkle with parmesan. Cover with foil and bake for 1 hour.

Remove the foil then return the dish to the oven for 5 minutes to brown the parmesan.

Serve with steamed or boiled green beans and crusty bread.

Tuna macaroni

serves 4

This pasta dish is quick and easy to prepare for the family; it can also be a great snack for hungry children and teenagers after school. Tuna is high in omega 6, and this dish is excellent for dry skin, arthritis and weak digestion. Parmesan adds flavour and is high in calcium.

400 g macaroni

1 × 375 g can tuna in oil, drained

1 tablespoon butter

2 tablespoons grated parmesan

sea salt and freshly cracked black pepper, to taste

Bring a large saucepan of salted water to the boil. Add the macaroni and boil for 5 minutes or until al dente.

While the pasta is cooking, in a bowl combine the tuna, butter and parmesan.

Drain the pasta and then return it to the saucepan. Add the tuna mixture and stir gently to combine. Season with salt and pepper and serve.

Spinach and rice

serves 4–6

This dish is wonderfully gentle for those with an upset stomach, heartburn or anaemia. Spinach is high in vitamin A, folic acid and contains some calcium, magnesium and other trace minerals. Rice is gluten-free and helps to line the stomach. Children and teenagers also enjoy this dish and you can make it a complete meal by serving it with fish, chicken or legumes.

1½ tablespoons extra-virgin olive oil

½ bunch spring onions, chopped

1 bunch fresh dill, chopped

1 bunch coarse spinach, washed and shredded with coarse stems removed

3½ cups water

1 cup long-grain rice (white or brown)

sea salt and freshly cracked black pepper, to taste

juice of 1 lemon

Add the oil to a saucepan over a low heat. Add the spring onion and dill and sauté for 5 minutes. Add the spinach and 1 cup water and stir for 2 minutes. Add remaining water and the rice and season with salt and pepper. Increase heat to medium and cook for 15 minutes. Remove the saucepan from the heat and cover with a tight-fitting lid. Leave to steam in its juices for 5 minutes for white rice or 15–20 minutes for brown rice, then pour over the lemon juice and serve.

Chicken and vegetable casserole

serves 4

The whole family will love this dish – and so will the cook, as the oven does all the work. If you like, add some broccoli to the casserole 10 minutes before it is ready, or steam some green vegetables while the casserole is cooking. For variety you can add some chopped ginger, or 1–2 teaspoons chopped rosemary or some fresh basil leaves.

4 free-range chicken breasts

4 carrots, roughly chopped

2 large onions, cut into 6–8 wedges

3 cloves garlic, chopped

4 medium potatoes, washed and cut into quarters

4 tomatoes, cut into 4–6 wedges

½ cup olive oil

1½ cups water

1 teaspoon sea salt

½ teaspoon freshly cracked black pepper

1–2 tablespoons chopped fresh parsley

1 tablespoon chopped ginger (optional)

Preheat oven to 190°C.

Arrange the chicken, carrot, onion, garlic, potato and tomato in a large baking dish. Splash with oil and then add the water. Sprinkle salt and pepper over the casserole, cover, and then bake for 1 hour, turning the meat and vegetables regularly.

Serve on its own or with green vegetables and perhaps some Couscous (see page 90) or Brown Rice (see page 93).

Jamie's osso bucco with parsnip mash

serves 2

This dish is from my nephew, Jamie Sach. It is a great winter dish for men and women who need iron for energy to play sport and exercise – and who like something tasty and healthy. Parsnips are an underrated root vegetable, and whether roasted or mashed with potato, they benefit the spleen and pancreas (excellent for diabetics) and are high in silicon, which helps to strengthen hair and nails.

2 thick slices beef shin (osso bucco cut)

4 tablespoons plain flour

sea salt and freshly cracked black pepper, to taste

olive oil, for frying

1 large leek, washed and thickly sliced

2 medium carrots, finely chopped

2 sticks celery, finely chopped

2 tablespoons olive oil

1–1.5 litres beef stock

140 g crushed tomatoes

1 small handful parsley, chopped

2 bay leaves

4 medium parsnips

4 medium waxy potatoes

1 knob butter or margarine

Preheat the oven to 180°C.

Score the edge of the beef shin in several places – this prevents it from contracting when it cooks. Season the flour in a bowl and toss the beef in it until well coated. Heat a little oil in a shallow frying pan, then add the beef shins and cook until lightly browned. Transfer to a plate.

Add the leek, carrot and celery to an oiled frying pan. Fry until the vegetables soften just a little, then transfer them to a heavy casserole dish. Place the browned beef shins on top and then add just enough stock to cover all the ingredients. Add the tomatoes, parsley and bay leaves and season with plenty of salt and pepper. Cover and bake for 2–3 hours; when the meat falls from the bone it is ready.

To prepare the mash, peel and roughly chop the parsnip and potato into equally sized pieces. Bring them to the boil in a saucepan of water with a pinch of salt. Once soft, drain the vegetables well and add the butter/margarine. Season with salt and pepper and roughly mash – it's nice if it still has a little texture.

Serve the osso bucco on the bed of parsnip mash with a green vegetable of your choice – in my house peas are always a winner!

Barramundi, lemon and potato

serves 4

This is a dish for the whole family. Serve with Rice Salad (see page 54) or Couscous Salad (see page 64) or three steamed vegetables such as spinach, carrots and squash.

4 medium kipfler potatoes (or other waxy potatoes), cut into cubes

½ green capsicum, deseeded and chopped into small cubes

½ red capsicum, deseeded and chopped into small cubes

4 fillets barramundi or pearl perch (180–200 g per fillet)

juice of 2 lemons

sea salt, to taste

1 tablespoon chopped fresh parsley

Preheat oven to 180°C.

Parboil the potatoes for 5–10 minutes until tender. Drain.

In a medium ovenproof dish add the potato and capsicums, then top with the fish fillets. Pour over the lemon juice and season with salt. Bake for 15–20 minutes or until the fish is cooked through.

Remove from the oven and sprinkle over the parsley.

Butterfly zucchini pasta

serves 4

This is a wonderful dish that I often serve as a dinner-party entrée or when I feel like a lighter meal. If serving as a light meal, add a lentil or chickpea salad on the side.

400 g fresh farfalle (butterfly-
  shaped) pasta

2 tablespoons extra-virgin olive oil

1 medium onion, finely chopped

2 cloves garlic, chopped

2 zucchini, finely sliced

sea salt and freshly cracked
  black pepper, to taste

grated parmesan, to serve

freshly chopped parsley, to serve

Bring a large saucepan of salted water to the boil. Add the pasta and boil for 6 minutes or until al dente.

While the pasta is cooking, heat the oil in a frying pan and place over medium heat. Add the onion, garlic and zucchini and sauté for 2 minutes or until the onion and zucchini begin to brown, then remove from heat.

Drain the pasta and return it to the saucepan. Mix the zucchini sauce through the pasta and season with salt and pepper. Stir some parmesan and parsley through and serve.

Jamie's Thai beef salad

serves 2

*My nephew Jamie Sach's Thai beef salad contains a wonderful mix of vita-
mins. Beef is high in vitamin B, folic acid and iron. All the vegetables are high
in vitamins A and C, and the coriander and mint aid digestion of the meat and
help cleanse the liver. Basil is a herb known to 'lift the spirits'.*

1 sirloin steak, fat trimmed

2 tablespoons white rice

coriander sprig, to serve

Dressing

2 cloves garlic, finely chopped

1 small piece lemongrass, finely chopped

1 small piece galangal (Thai ginger),
   finely chopped (or ordinary ginger)

1 tablespoon sesame oil

juice of 1 lemon

2 tablespoons fish sauce

1 tablespoon white vinegar

Salad

4 spring onions, finely sliced julienne

1 medium red onion, finely sliced
   julienne

1 medium carrot, finely sliced
   julienne

1 small red capsicum, deseeded
   and finely sliced julienne

1 small green/yellow capsicum,
   deseeded and finely sliced julienne

1 stick celery, finely sliced julienne

1 bunch fresh coriander, washed
   and patted dry, leaves picked
   and roughly chopped

1 bunch fresh mint, washed and
   patted dry, leaves picked and
   roughly chopped

1 bunch fresh Thai basil, washed
   and patted dry, leaves picked
   and roughly chopped

To make the dressing, combine the ingredients (I like to use a lot of fish sauce, but season to taste – it is quite salty) in a small bowl and mix well. Set aside while you prepare the steak and salad.

Cook the steak on a preheated grill to medium-rare. Remove from heat and set aside to rest.

Place the rice in a dry frying pan and cook over a medium-hot heat until the rice begins to turn toasty brown. Transfer the rice to a mortar and grind it coarsely using a pestle.

To make the salad, place all the ingredients in a large salad bowl and combine well.

Slice the steak into thin ribbons and toss with the vegetables and then add the dressing. Lastly, toss though the crunchy toasted rice. Serve with a sprig of coriander on top.

Spaghetti with garlic, oil and chilli

serves 4

This is a very quick and easy dish to make if you are hungry and need something tasty, light and clean to the palate. It is excellent for those with sensitive stomachs and also teenagers who are hungry during their study time.

400 g fresh spaghetti

2–3 tablespoons extra-virgin olive oil

4 cloves garlic, chopped

1 fresh chilli, finely chopped

½ bunch fresh parsley, chopped

1 handful parmesan, grated

sea salt and freshly cracked black pepper, to taste

Bring a large saucepan of water to the boil. Add the spaghetti and boil for 6 minutes or until al dente.

While the spaghetti is cooking, heat the oil in a frying pan and place over medium heat for 30 seconds or until the oil is hot. Add the garlic and sauté for 1 minute, then add the chilli and sauté until the garlic is just brown.

Drain the spaghetti and return it to the saucepan. Add the oil and garlic mixture and stir to combine. Add the parsley and parmesan, then season with pepper and salt, stir and serve.

Whole baked snapper

serves 2

Snapper is high in most nutrients, especially vitamin A for dry and flaky skin. This is an easy dish to prepare after a long day at the office, especially on a hot summer evening. Serve with a green salad or steamed vegetables or new potatoes.

2 medium snapper, cleaned and scaled

1 medium onion, finely sliced

1 medium tomato, finely sliced

1 clove garlic, chopped

juice and grated rind of 1 lemon

rock salt and freshly cracked
   black pepper, to taste

butter, for baking

1 fresh red chilli, finely chopped
   (optional)

Preheat oven to 180°C.

Rinse the fish under running water and dab dry with paper towel.

Place two large sheets of foil on a baking tray and place each fish on a sheet of foil. Arrange slices of onion, tomato and garlic over each fish and then sprinkle the lemon rind over. Pour the lemon juice over the top and season with salt and pepper. Add a dob of butter to the top of each fish and chilli (if using). Fold foil around the fish so each is enclosed in its own parcel, and bake for 20 minutes. To test whether the fish is cooked, use a fork to gently pull a small part of the flesh away. If the flesh is white and tender, the fish is ready. Serve with Jacket Potatoes (see page 82).

Tofu and shiitake mushroom stir-fry

serves 2

This is especially good for those with a lowered immune system. Shiitake mushrooms are a natural source of interferon, a protein that stimulates a positive immune response. They are also known for their ability to lower levels of cholesterol and fats in the blood.

Tofu is very digestible, high in B vitamins and minerals, and is inexpensive and low in kilojoules, as well as being a valuable source of calcium for children, nursing mothers and menopausal women. It should be stored in an airtight container in the refrigerator and covered with water; change the water daily. It can be baked, steamed or sautéed and added for a light protein to any vegetable dish.

3 dried shiitake mushrooms

1 cup water

1 tablespoon peanut oil

2 tablespoons sesame oil

1 cup raw or frozen (defrosted)
   fresh green peas

1 carrot, grated

1 small onion, chopped (optional)

200 g tofu, cut into small cubes

½ teaspoon rock salt

2 teaspoons soy sauce

1 tablespoon sesame oil

freshly cracked black pepper,
   to taste

Soak the mushrooms in the water for 20–30 minutes, then drain, retaining the strained soaking water. Discard the mushroom stalks and thinly slice the mushroom cups.

Pour the peanut and sesame oil into a frying pan over a medium-high heat and add the mushrooms. Sauté for 2 minutes, then add the peas, carrot and onion (if using). Add half of the soaking water and cook for 5 minutes on high.

Add the tofu cubes to the cooked vegetables, then the rest of the soaking liquid, salt, soy sauce and sesame oil. Cook for a further 5–10 minutes (do not break the tofu cubes) stirring once or twice.

Season with pepper and serve on rice or with a green salad.

Kebabs

serves 4

This is a great dish on the barbecue for eating outdoors in summer. Serve with a green salad for extra nutrition and colour.

your favourite vegetables, such as
   1 green capsicum, 1 squash,
   1 large mushroom, 1 tomato,
   1 zucchini, 1 eggplant, all cut
   into chunks

8 bamboo skewers, soaked in cold
   water for 20 minutes (this will prevent
   them from burning on the barbecue)

100 g fetta, cut into large cubes
1 free-range chicken breast fillet,
   cut into large cubes

1 piece flake or pearl perch, cut
   into large cubes

½ cup extra-virgin olive oil

sea salt and freshly cracked
   black pepper, to taste

4 sprigs fresh mint, ½ bunch
   fresh basil or ½ bunch dried
   oregano, chopped

Tahini (see page 80) or Simple
   Tomato Sauce (see page 91),
   to serve

Lightly brush the vegetables, cheese, chicken and fish with oil, then season with salt and pepper. Thread them onto the skewers, alternating ingredients, and then sprinkle with the herbs and chilli (if using). Grill the skewers on a hot plate or barbecue, turning, for 15 minutes or until the chicken and fish are cooked and brown. Serve with Tahini or Simple Tomato Sauce.

Fish with soy sauce and ginger

serves 2

This is a great recipe for the whole family. I often make this dish after work because it is quick and easy. Ginger helps digestion, but you can substitute some parsley or coriander or finely chopped garlic if you prefer. Tamari is a wheat-free soy sauce, which can be bought in a health store. Look for salt-reduced soy sauces if you suffer fluid retention or cardiovascular disease.

2 fillets mahi mahi or your
   favourite boneless fish

1 teaspoon finely chopped fresh
   ginger root

2 tablespoons tamari

juice of 1 lemon

2 tablespoons olive oil

Cut the fish into 2-cm squares. In a bowl, combine the ginger, tamari and lemon juice. Add the fish and allow it to marinate for 30 minutes.

Heat the oil in a frying pan over medium heat. Add the fish and marinade and cook, stirring gently, for 5–8 minutes or until the flesh is white and soft.

Serve on a bed of Couscous (see page 90) or Mashed Potato (see page 92) and a salad of freshly chopped rocket.

Roast spatchcock

serves 4

Rosemary or honey can be used instead of garlic to flavour the spatchcock. For a single person, cooking one spatchcock as a mini-roast is great – you can leave it to cook while you go for a run.

4 free-range spatchcock

4 cloves garlic, chopped

4 medium potatoes, peeled and halved

2 carrots, halved and then sliced lengthways

1 onion, quartered

1 small sweet potato or 200 g pumpkin, peeled and roughly chopped

1 parsnip, peeled, halved and then sliced lengthways

2–3 tablespoons olive oil

sea salt and freshly cracked black pepper

2 tablespoons chopped parsley, to garnish

Preheat oven to 180°C.

You may choose to leave the spatchcock whole or you can use poultry scissors to cut along the breastbone to flatten, giving 2 halves per serve (children may only need half this).

Arrange the spatchcock, garlic, potato, carrot, onion, sweet potato or pumpkin and parsnip in a large baking dish. Sprinkle the oil over the spatchcock and vegetables and then season with salt and pepper.

Bake for 1–1½ hours, turning the spatchcock and vegetables 2–3 times so that they cook evenly.

When the spatchcock and vegetables are cooked (to test the spatchcock, insert a skewer into the thickest part of the leg – if the juices run clear and there is no blood, the spatchcock is ready), increase the oven temperature to 250°C for 5 minutes, to brown the potatoes.

Remove the baking dish from the oven and drain the spatchcock and vegetables on paper towel. Serve garnished with parsley.

Vegetable rissoles

makes 12 rissoles

Rissoles are a great way to encourage the family to eat a range of vegetables. Potato is a great base to start with, but you can also try rice or buckwheat if you are feeling a little more adventurous.

If you have leftover vegetables in your refrigerator at the end of the week, rissoles are a good way of using them up – be creative! Tahini (see page 80) can be added for extra taste, as well as herbs such as basil or thyme.

4 medium potatoes, peeled and cut into quarters

200 g pumpkin, peeled and cut into quarters

240 g frozen peas

1 teaspoon unsalted butter

olive oil

1 medium onion, finely chopped

2 zucchini, finely chopped

2 medium carrots, finely chopped

2 free-range eggs, beaten

1 cup fresh wholemeal breadcrumbs

3 tablespoons chopped fresh parsley

1 teaspoon sea salt

Place the potatoes and pumpkin in a large saucepan and cover with water. Bring to the boil over high heat, then reduce heat to low and simmer for 15 minutes or until the potatoes and pumpkin are cooked. (You may prefer to steam the vegetables.)

Meanwhile, place the peas in a separate saucepan and cover with water. Bring to the boil over high heat and cook for 5–10 minutes or until the peas are soft.

Drain potatoes, pumpkin and peas and combine in a large mixing bowl. Add the butter and mash the vegetables together.

Add a little oil to a large frying pan over medium heat. Add the onion, zucchini and carrot and sauté for 5 minutes. Transfer the mixture to the bowl of mashed vegetables, then add the eggs, parsley and salt and mix well. When the mixture is cool enough to handle, shape it into patties with your hands, then roll them in breadcrumbs to thoroughly coat. Refrigerate the rissoles for 1 hour.

Preheat oven to 180°C.

Place the rissoles on an oven tray lined with baking paper and bake for 30–40 minutes or until brown. (You may prefer to pan-fry the rissoles for 5 minutes on each side.) Serve with your favourite salad.

Chicken drumsticks

Here are my two favourite recipes for chicken legs, which make a great snack for children when they get home from school or served cold as part of their school lunch, and also for parties when you are feeding 10 or 20 people. You can also serve these with Jacket Potatoes (see page 82) or Caesar Salad (see page 66) or any other salad.

Honey soy chicken drumsticks

serves 4

½ cup soy sauce

½ cup honey

8 free-range chicken drumsticks
  (2 per person)

1–2 tablespoons sesame seeds
  (optional)

1–2 tablespoons pumpkin seeds
  or cashew nuts (optional)

Preheat oven to 180°C.

In a jug combine the soy sauce and honey. Place the chicken drumsticks in a large baking dish and pour the marinade over them.

Transfer the chicken drumsticks to a baking dish and sprinkle over the sesame seeds, pumpkin seeds and cashew nuts (if using). Bake, turning the chicken drumsticks every 15 minutes, for 1 hour, or until they are crisp and brown.

Chicken drumsticks with rosemary and chilli

serves 4

1½ cups dry white wine

3 cloves garlic, chopped

1 tablespoon fresh rosemary

½ teaspoon chilli flakes or powder

8 free-range chicken drumsticks
(2 per person)

¼ bunch parsley, finely chopped

Preheat oven to 180°C.

In a jug combine the wine, garlic, rosemary and chilli. Place the chicken drumsticks in a large baking dish, pour the marinade over and cover the dish with foil.

Bake the chicken drumsticks, turning them every 15 minutes, for 30 minutes and then remove the foil and bake for a further 30 minutes, or until they are crisp and brown. Sprinkle the parsley over the chicken to serve.

Butter bean rissoles

serves 2–4

The butter bean is a complete protein that strengthens the liver and lungs, and is also high in potassium and folic acid, and has no cholesterol. Lima beans are great for heartburn, an irritable bowel and arthritis.

2 free-range eggs, beaten

1 cup fresh breadcrumbs

1 large potato, peeled and boiled

1 medium onion, finely chopped

1 medium carrot, finely chopped

2 sticks celery, finely chopped

1 × 400 g can butter beans, drained and mashed

sea salt and freshly cracked black pepper, to taste

vegetable oil, for cooking

2 tablespoons finely chopped fresh mint or parsley

Place the eggs and breadcrumbs in separate bowls.

In a large bowl combine the potato, onion, carrot, celery, and butter beans. With a masher (or a fork) mash the ingredients and season with salt and pepper.

With wet hands, shape the mixture into patties, then dip each in the egg and roll in the breadcrumbs to thoroughly coat.

Add a little vegetable oil to a frying pan over low heat and cook the rissoles for 2–3 minutes on each side or until brown. Sprinkle with mint or parsley and serve with a rocket or tomato salad.

Lamb and lentils on a bed of mashed potato

serves 4

This is an excellent protein dish for sportspeople, those recovering from illness, or those who need extra body warmth in winter. It is high in iron (from the lamb), minerals (from the lentils) and is very tasty.

extra-virgin olive oil, for cooking

1 large onion, roughly chopped

500 g minced lamb

1 medium green capsicum, deseeded and roughly chopped

1 × 400 g can diced tomatoes

1 cup red lentils

3 cups water or Vegetable Stock (see page 75)

2 teaspoons chilli paste (optional)

3 teaspoons mixed dried herbs

sea salt and freshly cracked black pepper, to taste

1 serve Mashed Potato (see page 92)

Heat a little oil in large saucepan over low heat. Add the onion and cook until it is translucent and soft. Add the lamb a little at a time, constantly stirring to break up any lumps. When all the lamb is browned, add the capsicum, tomatoes, lentils, water, chilli and herbs. Season with salt and pepper, then simmer for 35 minutes.

Serve on a bed of mashed potato with a mixed green salad on the side.

Prawns with Asian herbs

serves 4

This is an excellent summer dish, particularly for those watching their weight and who are changing from heavier meat dishes to lighter foods.

1 kg raw prawns

juice of 2 limes

1 stick lemongrass, chopped

1 tablespoon grated fresh ginger

½ fresh chilli, chopped (optional)

½ teaspoon ground turmeric

½ teaspoon ground cumin

1 handful fresh coriander, chopped

2 cups jasmine or basmati rice

2 tablespoons vegetable oil

1 × 325 g can light coconut milk

Shell the prawns, leaving the tails intact. In a large bowl combine the lime juice, lemongrass, ginger, chilli, turmeric, cumin and coriander. Add the prawns, mix well and leave to marinate for 10–15 minutes.

Bring a large saucepan of water to the boil. Add the rice and boil for 10–15 minutes or until just soft.

While the rice is cooking, heat the oil in a deep frying pan over medium heat. Add the prawns and their marinade and cook for 4–5 minutes or until the prawns are pink. Add the coconut milk and stir to heat through. Taste and add more lime juice if necessary. Strain the rice and arrange in serving bowls, and serve the prawns and sauce over the rice.

Salmon rice rissoles

serves 4

These rissoles are a good balance of protein and carbohydrate. The omega 3 oils assist brain development and healthy skin in children, and in adults they benefit arthritis and high cholesterol. You can use tuna if you prefer.

1 cup fresh breadcrumbs

1 × 400 g can salmon, drained

juice of ½ lemon

1 medium onion, finely chopped

3 cups cooked Brown Rice (see page 93)

2 free-range eggs, beaten

1 large carrot, grated

vegetable salt, to taste

2 tablespoons extra-virgin olive oil

Place the breadcrumbs in a large bowl.

In a separate bowl combine the salmon, lemon juice, onion, rice, egg and carrot, and season with vegetable salt. Mix well and then, using wet hands, shape the mixture into patties, then roll in breadcrumbs.

Heat the oil in a large frying pan over low–medium heat. Add the patties and cook for 5 minutes on each side or until light brown on the outside. Place the patties on paper towel to drain any excess oil before serving them with a Mixed Salad with Nuts (see page 58) or a salad of your choice.

Spaghetti vongole

serves 4

Spaghetti vongole is light and tasty, and is delicious for lunch with a salad on a hot summer day. It is also especially delicate on the stomach if you are recovering from a big night out. Clams are a light protein.

400 g fine spaghetti

½ cup extra-virgin olive oil

1 medium onion, chopped

3 cloves garlic, finely chopped

1 kg baby clams, soaked in a bowl of cold water for 1 hour before cooking

2 glasses dry white wine

2 tablespoons freshly chopped parsley

sea salt and ½ teaspoon freshly cracked black pepper

Bring a large saucepan of salted water to the boil. Add the spaghetti and boil until al dente.

While the spaghetti is cooking, heat the oil in a large frying pan and place over medium heat. Add the onions and garlic and sauté for 1 minute or until brown. Add the clams and wine, cover and cook for 5–10 minutes or until the clams open, then add the parsley and season with salt and pepper. Discard any clams that do not open.

Drain the spaghetti and place in serving bowls, then pour over the clams and cooking juices.

Soy chicken and potatoes

serves 4

This meal is simple, nutritious and tasty.

2 cloves garlic, crushed

⅓ cup soy sauce

4 free-range chicken breast fillets

1 handful pumpkin seeds
  (optional)

2 teaspoons sesame seeds
  (optional)

4 medium potatoes, peeled (or
  just washed) and quartered, or
  8 new baby potatoes, washed
  with skins on

2 tablespoons olive oil

sea salt and freshly cracked
  black pepper, to taste

In a large bowl combine the garlic and soy sauce. Add the chicken and
seeds (if using) and mix well to thoroughly coat the chicken, and set
aside to marinate for 20 minutes.

Preheat oven to 180°C.

Transfer the chicken to a medium baking dish and pour over
the remaining marinade. Add the potatoes and sprinkle them with
oil (for flavour and to allow them to brown while cooking). Bake for
45 minutes.

When the chicken and potatoes are cooked, season with salt and
pepper and serve with steamed peas, beans and carrots.

Pumpkin and sage pasta

serves 4

This dish makes a hearty meal with a salad on the side. Pumpkin is high in anti-oxidants and sage is a wonderful herb for menopausal women, because it balances the drop in oestrogen, helping to lift the spirits. There is no protein, so for those wishing to lose weight, add almonds (protein) to your side salad (see Chickpea and Avocado Salad on page 61 and Couscous Salad on page 64).

400 g penne

500 g pumpkin, peeled and cut into 2-cm cubes

sea salt and freshly cracked black pepper, to taste

½ cup olive oil

2 teaspoons butter

3 leeks, washed, trimmed and thinly sliced

1 bunch fresh sage, washed and leaves picked

Vegetable Stock (see page 75) or water (optional)

2 tablespoons grated parmesan

4 tablespoons fresh ricotta

fresh peas or fresh young cooked beans (optional)

Preheat oven to 180°C.

Bring a large saucepan of salted water to the boil. Add the pasta and boil for 8 minutes or until the pasta is al dente.

While the pasta is cooking, place the pumpkin cubes on an oven tray and sprinkle with salt, pepper and a little of the oil. Bake the pumpkin, turning regularly, for 20 minutes or until it is soft and browned.

Melt half the butter in a saucepan. Add the leek and fry until the leek is soft, then add the remaining butter and the sage leaves, and increase heat until the sage leaves curl and become crisp.

Drain the pasta and then return it to the saucepan. Add remaining oil and the leek–sage mixture. (If the pasta is too dry, add a little stock or water.) Stir in the parmesan and season with salt and pepper. Place the pasta in serving bowls and top with the baked pumpkin, dollops of fresh ricotta and fresh peas or beans (if using).

Pearl perch with Corn Flakes crusty coating

serves 4

A perfect lighter meal in the evening and for summer, this is excellent for weight loss and joint problems. Children love eating fish cooked this way – it is quick, easy and tasty.

2 free-range eggs, beaten

3 cups Corn Flakes

4 pearl perch fillets, pin-boned

1–2 tablespoons olive oil

2 tablespoons finely chopped fresh parsley

Place the beaten eggs in a bowl. Place the Corn Flakes in a separate bowl and crush coarsely.

Use paper towel to dry the perch. Dip each fillet into the egg, then roll in the Corn Flakes, coating thoroughly.

Heat the oil in a frying pan over low–medium heat for 10–20 seconds. Add the perch fillets and fry for 4–5 minutes on both sides or until cooked and golden brown.

Garnish with parsley and serve with your favourite salad or vegetables.

Lamb casserole

serves 4

This warming casserole for autumn and winter is packed with goodness. It is especially good after a severe virus, flu or cold. The cooking juices are full of vital nutrients, B12, folic acid and iron from the meat.

2 medium carrots, roughly chopped

2 medium onions, roughly chopped

4 medium potatoes, peeled and roughly chopped

2 medium tomatoes, roughly chopped

2 medium zucchini (or a handful of green beans), roughly chopped

2 cloves garlic, finely chopped

1 teaspoon fresh rosemary leaves

8 lamb (leg) chops, excess fat removed

sea salt and freshly cracked black pepper, to taste

2 tablespoons olive oil

½ cup chopped broccoli and ½ cup chopped cauliflower (optional)

Preheat oven to 190°C.

Add all the vegetables, garlic, rosemary and chops to a baking dish. Sprinkle salt and pepper and pour over enough water to cover the meat and vegetables; about 1½ cups. Pour over the oil and then bake for 45 minutes. Remove from the oven and stir in the broccoli and cauliflower. Continue baking for a further 15–20 minutes.

Serve the casserole by itself or over Couscous (see page 90).

Kingfish with fresh mint sauce

serves 4

This is a very healthy and quick fish dish – I have found that men especially like this. It is excellent for weight loss, assists digestion, and the mint helps the break-down of the essential omega 3 fatty acids. You can also try this dish with marlin instead of kingfish.

4 kingfish fillets, pin-boned

1 teaspoon sea salt

2 tablespoons extra-virgin olive oil

2 large onions, chopped

2 bunches fresh mint leaves, chopped

2 tablespoons white-wine vinegar

Lightly spread salt evenly over both sides of the kingfish. Place the fish under a hot grill and cook for 3–5 minutes on each side.

As the kingfish is cooking, heat the oil in a frying pan over medium heat. Add the onion and mint, and sauté for 5 minutes or until the onion has caramelised. Add the white-wine vinegar.

Arrange the kingfish on serving plates, spoon the fresh mint sauce over, and serve with your favourite salad or vegetables.

Sweets

Apricot coconut balls

makes approximately 12

Like all dried fruit, these are very sweet and should be used only as a small treat. This recipe is not suitable for people suffering from hypoglycaemia or for those trying to lose weight. Apricots are high in copper and cobalt, which assist anaemia.

1 cup dried apricots (or dates or prunes)

1 teaspoon finely grated orange rind

½ teaspoon lemon juice

1 tablespoon orange juice

1 cup desiccated coconut

Soak the apricots in boiling water until they are soft, then drain and finely chop them and transfer them to a large bowl. Add the orange rind, lemon juice and orange juice and mix well. With your hands, form the mixture into small balls and then roll in coconut to coat. Serve immediately or store in an airtight container in the fridge for up to 7 days.

Baked sweet bananas with cinnamon

serves 4

This is one of my favourite desserts, especially on a cold winter evening. Bananas are gentle on the intestines, bowel and stomach. They help to detox the body and assist those with a 'sweet tooth' to stop eating chocolates and sweet junk food. Bananas are especially good for women with PMS who crave sugars. Bananas are rich in potassium and useful for those who play a lot of sport. Children usually love this dish. Cinnamon also warms the blood and assists in the digestion of the bananas.

4 bananas

2 tablespoons brown sugar

½ teaspoon ground cinnamon

¼ teaspoon ground nutmeg

juice and grated rind of 1 orange

1 tablespoon honey or golden syrup

juice and finely grated rind of
    1 lemon

2 tablespoons desiccated coconut

yoghurt or ice-cream, to serve

Preheat oven to 180°C.

Peel the bananas, slice them lengthways and place them in a baking dish.

In a small saucepan combine the sugar, cinnamon, nutmeg, orange juice and rind, honey or golden syrup, and the lemon juice and rind. Heat for a few minutes, then pour the syrup over the bananas.

Bake the bananas for approximately 15 minutes or until golden brown and soft, spooning over the syrup every 5 minutes. Remove from the oven and divide among serving plates. Sprinkle the coconut over the bananas and serve with yoghurt or ice-cream.

Poached pears

serves 4

The cooking process removes the acid and makes fruit very digestible. It is particularly good for the young and elderly with delicate digestive systems or joint problems, and for those with constipation, and bloating. I highly recommend homemade cooked fruit for women when they crave sugary snacks.

You can poach or stew any fruit, especially apples and stone fruit such as peaches, apricots and nectarines. You do not need to add sugar. (For fruits other than pears, the vanilla bean and cinnamon stick are optional.)

4 pears, peeled and quartered length-ways (or left whole if you prefer)

1 vanilla bean

1 cinnamon stick

yoghurt or ice-cream, to serve (optional)

Place the pears in a saucepan and cover them with water. Place the vanilla bean and cinnamon stick in the water and simmer for 15–20 minutes, or until soft. Discard the vanilla bean and cinnamon stick, and serve the poached pears plain or with yoghurt, soy ice-cream or a sprinkle of cinnamon.

Anzac biscuits

makes 20 biscuits

What would a nutritious recipe book be without the famous Australian Anzac biscuits that we were all brought up on? Anzac biscuits are delicious and filled with rolled oats, which help feed and strengthen the nervous system, and the natural sweetness of golden syrup. These are a far better snack for all the family than chocolate, lollies, fizzy drinks and sweet biscuits. Children love to take them to school as a recess snack.

1 cup organic rolled oats

¾ cup desiccated coconut

1 cup plain flour (you can use wholemeal, white or gluten-free flour)

1 cup brown sugar

125 g butter

1 heaped tablespoon golden syrup

2 tablespoons boiling water

1½ teaspoons bicarbonate of soda

Preheat oven to 160°C and line 2 oven trays with baking paper.

In a bowl combine the oats, coconut, flour and sugar and make a well in the centre.

In a saucepan combine the butter and golden syrup and place over low heat to melt. In a separate small bowl pour the boiling water onto the bicarbonate of soda to dissolve, then pour this mixture into the melted butter and golden syrup.

Pour the liquid mixture over the oats mixture and stir until combined. Place dobs of the mixture evenly on the oven trays and then flatten a little with your fingers. Bake for 20 minutes and then allow the biscuits to cool on the oven tray for a few minutes before transferring them to a wire rack to cool completely. You can keep left-overs stored in an airtight container for up to 2 weeks.

Baked apples and pears

serves 4

Baking or boiling fruit is one of the greatest ways to give your family healthy, satisfactory, sweet desserts that are not only easy on the digestion but will suit and satisfy all ages. Cooked fruits are especially wonderful in winter. They are useful for those who suffer heartburn, ulcers, constipation and also help to satisfy the sugar cravings of women with PMS.

1 heaped tablespoon raisins	1 tablespoon ground cinnamon
1 handful almonds, finely chopped	2 cups water
4 apples or pears, cored	yoghurt or soy ice-cream, to serve

Preheat oven to 180°C.

In a bowl combine the raisins and almonds. Stuff the apples or pears with the mixture and sprinkle with cinnamon. Place the fruit in a small baking dish and pour over the water. Bake for 20 minutes or until soft, then serve the fruit with yoghurt or soy ice-cream.

Index